George W. Bush and the 2007-08 Financial Crisis And A Brief History of America's Economic Development

by

Dan Ostrander

AMERICAN HISTORY
PRESIDENTIAL LEADERSHIP

PITTSBURGH, PENNSYLVANIA 15238

The contents of this work, including, but not limited to, the accuracy of events, people, and places depicted; opinions expressed; permission to use previously published materials included; and any advice given or actions advocated are solely the responsibility of the author, who assumes all liability for said work and indemnifies the publisher against any claims stemming from publication of the work.

DORRANCE
PUBLISHING CO
EST. 1920
PITTSBURGH, PENNSYLVANIA 15238

Dorrance Publishing Co
585 Alpha Drive
Pittsburgh, PA 15238
Visit our website at *www.dorrancebookstore.com*

ISBN: 979-8-89341-401-1
eISBN: 979-8-89341-900-9

Dedication

This book is dedicated to my wife, Dawn, who is also my best friend and has given me much love and support through the years.

Table of Contents

Introduction

During 2007-2008, George W. Bush, the 43rd President of the United States, was confronted with a Financial Crisis that could have shut down the U.S. and world economies causing a 1929 type depression. In response to the crisis, President Bush and members of his administration created the Troubled Asset Relief Program (TARP) and persuaded Congress to pass the program. His actions during this crisis caused him to be highly criticized for abandoning his free-market conservative economic ideas. As a result of this abandonment, and his subsequent actions, President Bush alienated his GOP base to deal with the country's financial problems. His actions and those of his successor, President Barack Obama, not only led to the Federal Government and the taxpayers recovering **$444,224,638,127 which included the TARP funding,** but also included interest and the administrative expenses for TARP. The Bush and Obama efforts also led to a profit of **$403,194,653,696** for the Federal Government and the taxpayers after spending **$31,466,373,316** in grants for affordable housing for those hardest hit by the Financial Crisis.

If Bush or any President falls prey to the political pressures within society and compromises what he believes to be right in his conscience, then he has failed himself, the office of the Presidency, and most important of all, he has failed the people who elected him to use his judgement to represent their interests—even if they disagree with his judgment. This line of thinking about leadership was first articulated by the British statesman, Edmund Burke, (1729-1797) when he said:

"It ought to be the happiness and glory of a representative to live in the strictest union, the closest correspondence, and the most unreserved communication with his constituents. Their wishes ought to have great weight with him: their enlightened conscience—they ought never to sacrifice to you—Your representative owes you not only his industry, but his judgment; and he betrays, instead of serving you, if he sacrifices it to your opinion." # 1

Not only did Bush have the integrity and character to carry out his responsibilities as he saw them, he also demonstrated three of the most important elements of presidential leadership as articulated by former President Richard Nixon: (1) Vision-- which direction to take the country, (2) the courage of his convictions, and (3) he was a pragmatist—which means he had a flexible vision and was not driven by ideology or party politics.

In evaluating Bush's leadership during the Financial Crisis there are three issues that need to be discussed.

1. First, explain how close the U.S. and the World economies were to a total collapse. The cause of the Financial Crisis was a long time in the making, but the public awareness of the Crisis started on September 15, 2008, when Lehman Brothers, with $639 billion in assets, filed the largest bankruptcy in U.S. history. Lehman tried to find a buyer and had hoped for government assistance to facilitate a deal, but the Treasury Department refused to intervene, citing "moral hazard". Lehman's failure created turmoil in financial markets worldwide. Less than two weeks later Washington Mutual, the country's largest savings and loan, was seized by federal regulators. These events as well as others created liquidity problems as markets froze in the U.S. and around the world. Over the next few months, the U.S. stock market plummeted, liquidity dried up and companies laid off thousands of employees---approximately 7.5 million jobs were lost between 2007-2009. Bush 43 realized that the well-being of Main Street was directly linked to Wall Street and as

president he needed to do whatever was necessary to pull the country out of the panic. Former Federal Reserve Chairman Ben Bernanke stated that in the beginning of the 2008 financial crisis a financial meltdown was a threat to 12 of the 13 most important financial institutions. Bernanke stated the United States was at risk of failure within a period of a few weeks. He further claimed the 2008 financial crisis was actually worse than its 1930s counterpart.

2. Explain the need to demonstrate the kind of pragmatic leadership this country needed in a time of crisis. Congress often chooses political interest over national interest. A president needs to educate the public and Congress about the difficulties and the complexities of the problems that need to be faced and what actions are best taken for the national interest. The office of the presidency is the only branch of government in a position to provide that leadership. Bush 43 with his leadership under the Troubled Asset Relief Program (TARP) provided the country with this type of leadership.
3. Finally, explain why Bush's decision to support TARP and his actions to intervene in the economy to preserve the free market was the right approach. By the time George W. Bush became President the "Perfect Storm" had gathered. All the events that created the conditions for the financial meltdown were present. The Financial Crisis would have occurred no matter who was president---it was just a matter of how and when.

The first of two early warning signs that the financial system was becoming unstable was the 1994 crash in residential mortgages. At that time three of the big producers and sellers of mortgage-back securities (MBS) Kidder Peabody, Bear Stearns,and Lehman Brothers all took big hits as the MBS market evaporated in 1994. For example, Kidder Peabody's mortgage company, owned by General Electric, was sold off in pieces to the highest bidders.

Another early warning sign that was triggered as a result of globalization was the 1998 Long-Term Capital Management (LTCM) crisis. The LTCM crisis was partly created by the events surrounding the Asian and Russian financial crises of the same year. These events will be discussed later under globalization.

Domestically and internationally, before George W. Bush became President, cracks in the financial system had already developed. Seven events that created new trends and behavior patterns which were **compounded by time,** over 32 plus years led to the 2007-2008 financial crisis. The interrelationship of these events and the complexity of their all-inclusive global relationship created a comfort zone that led to a worldwide culture of financial irresponsibility. The events were:

1. Congress produced a "Runaway Train" of legislation that involved 10 pieces of legislation between 1975-2007 that changed the way financial markets operated. The train load of legislation was based on ideology from both the left and the right that produced extremes in government policy.

2. The creation of new economic tools called CDO (Collateralized Debt Obligations), MBSs (Mortgage Back Securities), and CDSs or Credit Default Swaps ---which will be defined and explained later.

3. Globalization or the problem of not having or developing an international standard that contained the right balance between a bank's liquidity and its future losses. Tim Geithner said it best: "I believed then and still believe now that forcing banks to hold enough capital liquidity to absorb significant losses is the best defense against future crises, the ultimate shock absorber." # 2

4. Alan Greenspan and the Federal Reserve's policy of creating a low-interest rate environment and then losing control of that environment to the process of globalization.

5. The rating agencies and their practice of overrating securities in order to please their customers, maximize their profits and maintain their market share.

6. The human condition and its appetite for more, more, more—which spelled greed for Main Street and Wall Street.
7. The privatization of Freddie Mac and Fannie Mae combined with demands put on these GSEs (Government Sponsored Entities) by Congress to force the GSEs to meet affordable housing goals set annually by HUD: [1] the 2004 ruling by HUD that allowed high-risk loans to count toward the GSE's affordable housing goals that HUD REQUIRED and [2] in 2007 the percentage of affordable housing loans the GSE's were required to make was increased by HUD from 30% to 55%.

The complexity of the issues, the limited time in which a leader has to make the correct decision, and the lack of incomplete information available is a burden all Presidents must bear during a time of crisis. This was particularly true for President Bush during this Financial Crisis.

On September 18---three days after Lehman Brothers declared bankruptcy--- Bush 43 held a meeting with his economic team (the "gang of three": Secretary of the Treasury Hank Paulson, Federal Reserve Chairman Ben Bernanke, and SEC chairman Chris Cox) at the White House in the Roosevelt Room. At that meeting Federal Reserve Chairman Ben Bernanke "...raised the possibility of another Great Depression." # 3 Secretary of the Treasury Hank Paulson and SEC Chairman Chris Cox then laid out a four-point program to present to Congress to deal with the panic. The program would be called the Troubled Asset Relief Program (TARP) and would: (1) guarantee all money market deposits, (2) launch a new lending vehicle to restart the commercial paper market, (3) temporarily ban the short sale of leading financial stocks, and (4) purchase hundreds of billions of dollars in mortgage-backed securities.

Bush had to balance the social and economic needs of society against that of a free enterprise system. He had to balance and integrate the economic needs of a more complex financial system that was failing against the need to intervene in the free enterprise system in order to preserve the system.

What mattered most to Bush was people. His vision as expressed in his book, "Compassionate Conservatism" was that public service gave him as well as others the opportunity to provide an environment for people to have security and opportunity. Without vision, pragmatism is impotent and is nothing more than splitting the difference between extremes or taking the middle ground as an easy way out. Bush was not that kind of public servant who looked for the easy way out; he looked for the right way out. He made this clear in his September 18, 2008, White House conversation with his "gang of three" when he said: "Let's figure out the right thing to do and do it. I had made up my mind: The U.S. government was going all in." # 4

For the purpose of this discussion, Bush's action towards the Financial Crisis of 2007-08 will be classified as his **"all-in policy".** The **"all-in policy"** is credited not only with stabilizing the economy and bringing it back to life under TARP and the Treasury, but the policy is also responsible for the accomplishments of the Federal Reserve, the SEC as well the Federal Deposit Insurance Corporation (FDIC) working together to create liquidity for financial institutions. This was accomplished by providing non-recourse loan guarantees. Also, Bush's flexible vision was key in bringing the economy back to life. Bush delegated to his "gang of three" broad flexibility and responsibility for managing the financial crisis. As Keith Hennessey, one of President Bush's advisors, explained to me: "We were not quite sure what might happen next, or what other shoe might drop, and we knew we would have to adapt to changing circumstances, but we had the guidance and we understood the direction from the President." # 5

As President Bush had to make a conscious choice between what was politically correct, keeping the government out of the financial markets, and what was morally correct and required of him as President, subordinating his own views when he understood it was clearly in the national interest to do so. In his book Decision Points, he makes this point clear:

"The strategy was a breathtaking intervention in the free market. It flew against all my instincts. But it was necessary to pull the country out of the panic. I decided that the only way to preserve the free market in the long run was to intervene in the short run." # 6

Warren Buffett's comment about Bush 43 leadership seemed to agree that this type of political courage and political pragmatism is an essential ingredient of effective Presidential leadership. Warren Buffett said in November of 2010: "And though I never voted for George W. Bush, I give him great credit for leading, even as Congress postured and squabbled." # 7 At his conference in South Carolina in October of 2008, Bush made it clear that he only wanted to create the skeleton for the economic recovery. He said he would only spend part of the $700 billion from TARP, leaving the majority for his successor along with a sound, flexible and usable structure for the next administration. * (My wife and I attended the conference)

The next administration would be that of President Obama. Like President Bush, President Obama used the "gang of three" and the "all-in policy" to bring the country's economy back from the Financial Crisis. Under the Obama administration the "gang of three" included Federal Reserve Chairman Ben Bernanke, Secretary of the Treasury Timothy Geithner, and SEC Chairman Julius Genachowski from June 2009-March,2013.

Recovery from the Financial Crisis followed a three-stage process: (1) rescue, (2) recovery, and (3) rebuilding. The Bush administration and the "gang of three" dedicated most of their time and energy to rescue and a bit of time to recovery. Rebuilding the economy took place after the Bush Presidency and was carried out by the Obama administration. The Obama administration started the rebuilding process in July 2010 with the Dodd Frank law #8.

The leadership provided by President Bush during the financial crises, was not based on any single economic theory or ideology but rather a pragmatic balancing act between the needs of the nation and what he could get from Congress and the conservative wing of his own party. Bush 43 did not practice pragmatism as an end in it-self. For Bush it was only one tool used by him to create effective leadership to make the impossible possible to make a difference for the people and this nation.

Legendary investor Warren Buffett once said: The most consequential words in modern economics came from President George W. Bush. At the height of the 2008 Financial Crisis, Bush said: "If money isn't loosened up, this sucker could go down!" Buffet deemed this quip "the most important words in the history of economics." #9

President Bush was right; **liquidity** was the solution for bring the economy back to normal. The problem, as will be discussed was: (1) how do you determine the value of the financial assets as they were bundled up into MBS, CD, CDO, and CDS, and (2) after the Crisis how do you find the current owners of the financial assets in question as they were sliced and diced into many pieces and sold off, (3) which financial tools and financial institution or organization would be used to stabilize and help create value back to these assets, and (4) how do you restore confidence in the economy for Wall Street and Main Street.

The looming problem for Bush 43's Administration was the same as that faced by FDR during the Great Depression– fear. The result of the financial crisis could see investors fleeing to safety, banks hoarding liquidity, and creditors mistrusting counterparties. (A financial institution on either side of an interest rate swap or a currency, equity, or commodity swap.) In this climate of uncertainty, the public perception of the quality of mortgage-related assets mattered more than the actual quality of the assets. Firms with too many toxic assets could begin to lose their ability to borrow to meet their day-to-day financial needs, leading to fire sales further depressing prices of assets and forcing firms to take additional losses, intensifying this vicious cycle and exacerbating the concerns about liquidity in the financial markets. This process would lead to a vicious cycle that would spread from Wall Street to Main Street. The impact on Main Street would lead to a slowing economy by threatening jobs, retirement savings, small business loans and international trade, a lack of credit and purchasing power, that would have led to a feeling of panic throughout the economy.

The administration under the leadership of President Obama must be given credit for continuing to build on the foundation that

Bush 43 created. The combined efforts of Presidents Bush and Obama administrations saved the country from another 1929 like depression.

AIG is an example of how the failure of one major corporation could impact the entire economy and start the beginning of another great depression. AIG insured 180,000 businesses that employed two-thirds of the U.S. workforce. It also insured the health plans, property, vehicles, and retirement accounts of millions of Americans. Thus, the Bush administration was faced with two choices: (1) should the government not act for fear of creating a "moral hazard" and leave the stability of the entire economic system at risk or (2) lend AIG $182 billion to stabilize itself during the financial crisis.

The problem that most people did not understand, but Timothy Geithner, Obama's Secretary of the Treasury expressed quite well: "In these circumstances, you do not have perfect foresight. You're going to make mistakes, and you've got to decide which kind of mistakes are less damaging. It would be easier to correct the mistake of doing too much, I argued, than to escalate too slowly, let the situation burn out of control, and have to correct the mistake of doing too little. It made more sense to err on the side of averting a financial meltdown, than to buy insurance against a macroeconomic disaster." #10 Geithner later told a Senate committee that everyone was in on the decision within Bush's inter-circle; that the Federal Reserve (Fed) was going where it had not gone since the 1930's. We recognized, of course, that the use of this legal authority was, in itself, an extraordinary step. "At the same time, we were mindful that Congress included this lending power in the 1913 Federal Reserve Act for a reason, and it seemed irresponsible for us not to use that authority in this unique situation." The Federal Reserve Act of 1913 gave the power to the Fed to oversee monetary policy in order to keep the nation's economy on an even keel. #11

However, what people sometimes do not understand is that even though the Federal Reserve or Congress create new monetary policies or laws their impact does not occur right away. The new policies unfold over time as the requirements of the new policies or laws are implemented and trickle through the economic, social, or political structure of society. The **lag time** may take months and maybe even years.

This was the case with the **ten legislative acts** (which are explained in Section 1 below) **passed by Congress between 1975-2007.** The effects of these legislative acts and the new policies they created had lag time effects that were compounding and had delayed reactions as the Financial Crisis has shown.

Both in the short and long run intervention by Bush's administration was the right choice. Not everyone agreed; several of the twelve regional Federal Reserve Bank presidents strongly disagreed with TARP and Bernanke's market-by-market approach to the crisis. These presidents accused the Federal Reserve Board and Bernanke, "… of contributing to the turmoil by creating uncertainty and confusion about government policy and complained the Fed didn't have an "exit strategy"—a way to return to normal central banking when the Great Panic had subsided. # 12

Some of the criticism of TARP was justified as there were some serious shortcomings with the program. The biggest mistake by the Bush administration and the most obvious was not to put executive compensation restrictions on TARP recipients. To Main Street it appeared that TARP was a bailout of Wall Street. Also, a problem for many on Main Street was that executives who created the problems were NOT ever held personally or criminally accountable. The companies just paid a big fine and business continued as usual. Senate Finance Chairman Max Baucus wanted some executive compensation restrictions for TARP recipients but both Geithner and Paulson disagreed. Geithner stated: "…I was with Hank; I didn't think Congress should mess around with TARP as a way to reform executive compensation—not because I approved of the industry's lavish salaries and bonuses, but because reducing them seemed like a secondary objective in a crisis." # 13

Even though the Justice Department has levied billions of dollars in fines on big financial institutions like the $13.3 billion on JP Morgan Chase in 2013, the $16.6 billion on Bank of America in 2014 and the $7 billion on Citi in 2014 for the way they packaged and sold mortgage-backed securities; not ONE of their top executives has been held personally accountable financially or criminally. In April of 2016 after the Justice Department fined Goldman Sachs $5.06 billion over its conduct in the packaging and sale of residential mortgage-backed securities in the period leading up to the Financial Crisis, the Department declined to name a single individual at Goldman Sachs responsible for the misconduct. The lack of action by the Justice Department was despite a new policy directive issued in September 2015 that declared the DOJ would make "individual accountability" a centerpiece of its financial crime investigations. However, Benjamin Mizer, head of the Justice Department's Civil Division stated: "Today's settlement is another example of the department's resolve **to hold accountable those whose illegal conduct** resulted in the Financial Crisis of 2007- 2008." Mizer went on to state: "Viewed in conjunction with the previous multibillion-dollar recoveries that the department has obtained for similar conduct, this settlement demonstrates the pervasiveness of the banking **industry's fraudulent practices** in selling Residential Mortgage-Backed Security (RMBS), and the power of the Financial Institutions Reform, Recovery and Enforcement Act as a tool for combatting this type of wrongdoing." # 14

Public statements have been made that no one went to prison as a result of these financial crimes; that is not true. The people who did face criminal charges were associated with much smaller financial institutions. According to the Financial Institution Crimes and Fines Database 380 defendants have been convicted of a crime or received a fine for violations including bank fraud and mortgage fraud etc. Of those convicted 76 were bankers and 92 were bank borrowers. The people who did get convicted and fined were not CEOs from the major financial institution. However, the CEO and CFO of Country Bank of Massachusetts (Gregory Yates and Terrance Yates respectively) did get convicted. Other people from smaller financial institutions, who were also convicted were: Joseph DiValli, a loan officer who was sentenced to 1 year and 6 months in prison for wire fraud and a Title Agent Christopher Ju who was sentenced to 10 months in prison for committing fraud. U.S.

Bancorp chief operational risk officer Michael LaFontaine was personally fined $450,000 for his role in failing to prevent violations of U.S. anti-money laundering. # 15

The point Mizer and the Justice Department did not understand or didn't care about, is that these fraudulent practices had been going on for years before the Financial Crisis of 2007-2008 and that the $16,175,739,273 (see chart below) in finds leveed between 2002-2007 had no effects. **As the fines indicate, fraudulent practices and illegal conduct were present long before the Financial Crisis.** Although the Justice Department might have felt these fines would be sufficient to stop the fraudulent and illegal practices – they weren't. The Financial institutions were forced to pay huge fines in the course of negotiating a settlement. These fines were actually paid by the shareholders as Federal Agencies had developed a practice of the easy way out—no trail, no jail time, the company admits wrongdoing and they pay a fine. This has become an established pattern over the years and resulted in the financial company continuing to perform fraudulent practices and illegal conduct. **Between 2002-2007 financial institutions were fined well over $16 billion for mortgage and security fraud.** These fines in themselves should have been a red flag. But they weren't as the practice of no accountability, and fine paying continued even after the Financial Crisis as **$259 billion** in fines were paid between 2009-2019, would indicate. Worldwide **$321 billion** in fines were paid, of which U.S. banks paid **$259 billion**. # 16

A summary of the bank "settlements" fines between 2002-07 is as follows:

Bank of America / Merrill Lynch/ Countrywide	$3,456,950,000
Bear Stearns	$470,555,459
Goldman Sachs	$232,677,860
J. P. Morgan Chase	$4,810,000,000
Lehman Brothers	$130,000,000
CitiBank	$3,161,500,000
Morgan Stanley	$964,876,164

Credit Suisse	$251,475,000
AIG	$1,736,000,000
U.S. Bancorp Piper	$5,753,500
Jaffray Inc.	$32,500,000
UBS Warburg	$226,714,711
Bank One	$90,000,000
ABN AMRO Bank	$101,245,847
HSBC	$505,490,732
Total fines pre-Financial Crisis 2002-2006:	$16,175,739,273

A summary of settlement fines of the top 19 financial institutions for: 2008-2019

Bank of America/Merrill Lynch/ Countrywide	$80,167,679,375
JPMorgan Chase	$34,473,897,291
Citigroup	$25,513,956,855
Wells Fargo	$17,178,935,246
Deutsche Bank	$18,103,108,878
UBS	$16,795,249,409
Goldman Sachs	$12,147,272,639
NatWest Group PLC (RBS)	$13,457,904,000
BNP Paribas (French Bank)	$12,142,751,200
Credit Suisse	$10,720,635,126
Morgan Stanley	$9,818,866,234
Barclays	$5,961,708,033
HSBC	$4,093,551,444
Truist Financial (SunTrust)	$1,602,629,105
Bank of New York Mellon	$1,040,391,446
Credit Agricole (French)	$1,216,104,585
U.S. Bancorp	$1,231,981,099
UniCredit (Italian)	$1,312,536,632
State Street Corp	$1,100,247,124
Royal Bank of Canada	$933,034,885
Total fines from Financial Crisis:	$259,203,393,238*

The fines listed above have been taken from various sources, and the numbers have been adjusted to reflect **only those fines that have dealt with financial misconduct** that caused the 2007-2008 Financial Crisis. Fines that dealt with wage and labor issues, banking violations like money laundering (in some cases money laundering fines could have been added but they were not) and employment discrimination have been left out of the totals listed above. The **$259 billion** only includes fines from 2008 up to 2019. As indicated above there were another **$16 billion** in fines levied against financial institutions between 2002-2007 creating a total of **$275 billion** in fines against the top 20 financial institutions for fraud, toxic securities, and mortgage abuses. # 16

Although TARP was the right decision for the country, the public has failed to fully appreciate what TARP and the actions of Bush's **"all-in policy"** and the "gang of three" did to stabilize and improve the economy.

Chapter 1:

Seven Causes of the 2007-2008 Financial Crisis

Section: 1

Legislative Impact

The "**First Cause**" of the 2007-08 Financial Crisis can be found by looking at the economic impact of government policies between 1975-2007 established under the **Department of Housing and Urban Development** (HUD) and the **ten Congressional Legislative Acts** aimed at increasing home ownership among the "under-served or poor population." Both Democratic and Republican Congresses passed these ten legislative acts that were signed into law by BOTH Democratic and Republican Presidents.

Before the ten Congressional Legislative Acts were passed a process had developed that most financial institutions made mortgage loans and: (1) sold them to Fannie Mae to get new capital for additional loans and (2) held onto them until they matured. The loans purchased by Fannie Mae were securitized and then packaged into mortgage-back securities (MBS) and sold to investors in the secondary mortgage market. These loans were solid low risk AAA rated. The 10 Legislative Acts led to a high-risk environment that allowed many home loans to become subprime and led to "predatory lending" practices which helped lead to the Financial Crisis.

Actions by HUD and Congressional Legislation acts passed between 1975-2007 served as a catalyst to activate a basic weakness of the human condition---GREED by Main Street and Wall Street. The Congressional acts built the "Runaway Train" and greed pushed the train down the steep slope into a Financial Crisis. Greed was a **key element** in building the foundation for the Financial Crisis. The greed combined with the economic opportunities provided by government policies led to abuses and bad economic decisions by both Main Street and Wall Street. The economic opportunities became exacerbated by the process of globalization that not only spread the positive and negative effects of economic prosperity worldwide but also intertwined the major economies of the world and made them economically interdependent. As we will see, the intertwining process created by globalization made it difficult for individual countries to control and/or stabilize their own economies. Because the subprime mortgage mess was made in America, the U.S. government would be forced to lead the cleanup. In order to avoid a crisis in confidence and the collapse of financial institutions and economies worldwide that would follow; President Bush and his financial team would need to make decisions quickly and without the benefit of much historical perspective. Speed in decision making was also important because the U.S. economy had become so dependent on the daily flow of foreign money from abroad. Hence, deferring final decisions or avoiding public statements to preserve future political wiggle room was not an option. Thus, as mentioned, Bush delegated to Secretary of the Treasury Hank Paulson and Federal Reserve Chairman Ben Bernanke almost unconditional responsibility for managing the Financial Crisis. Because Paulson and Bernanke were chartering new territory it would be difficult for anyone in the Bush administration or any administration to explain to the public what was happening or offer a clear detailed explanation of what they were going to do.

In a 2008 interview, Paulson said, not once has Bush overruled him. "I've got a boss," he explained, who "understands that when you're dealing with something as unprecedented and fast-moving as this, we need to have a different operating style." #1 **This point became apparent to my wife and myself at President Bush's retreat in South Carolina as he discussed his approach to the Financial Crisis in October of 2008**. He made it clear that he would be flexible and adjust to the changes in the economic environment as needed.

The **Congressional Legislative Acts** passed in 1975, led to the development of the perfect storm and created a change in social philosophy and lending practices. The law was entitled: **The Home Mortgage Disclosure Act** (HMDA). The Act passed by a Democratic Congress and signed into law by a Republican President Gerald R. Ford-- required lending institutions to report their loan data. The significance of the act was that by 1977 the HDMA provided Congress with the information it needed to conclude discrimination was taking place in the housing market because lending institutions were not making loans to the "under-served or poor population" in communities where they had operating branches. A practice called "redlining." Members of Congress felt that "redlining" created racial isolation and undercut black wealth creation, accelerated ghettoization, and walled off black families in the urban communities that exploded into the riots of the 1960's. # 2

As a result of the data provided by HMDA and the conclusions reached by a Democratic Congress about the impacts of "redlining" a **second act** by Congress called **The Community Reinvestment Act (CRA** was signed into law by President Jimmy Carter in 1977. The act prohibits financial instructions from targeting only wealthier neighborhoods with their services. The CRA's stated purpose was to provide credit and thus housing opportunities to **"under-served or poor populations". The law provided penalties for lending institutions that did not make loans in low and moderate-income neighborhoods.** The law also created what can be called the **"clean hands doctrine"**, which emphasized that an institution's CRA activities should be undertaken in a safe and sound manner and does not require institutions to make high-risk loans that may bring losses to the institutions. Congress's failure to refuse to acknowledge the reality of making high risk loans in existing poor communities helped lay the foundation to the Financial Crisis. **Because the Legislative Acts stated that institutions should not make high-risk loans that may bring losses to the institutions; Congress could now claim "clean hands"**—they could now say banks just made poor decisions. But an institution's compliance record to the 1977 CRA was taken into account by the banking regulatory agencies when an institution was seeking to expand through merger, acquisition or branching. With the passage of the HMDA and the CRA the foundation was laid and an argument was developed for a need to change lending standards. **The key question is: why would banks lend money to people who had a subprime credit rating or could not afford to repay them?** The short answer is, they didn't and wouldn't until Congress passed a series of laws that strongly encouraged and, in some cases, mandated it. **The changes that were made between 1975 and 2007 were more than a subtle shift in lending practices; they were an abdication of the traditional lending standards that had existed for a century.** Before 1975 homebuyers who fell into today's subprime category would have been denied credit. The new standard created by Congress, would now force lending institutions to provide an opportunity for individuals with subprime credit to be eligible for home loans.

The CRA had two results: (1) banks closed branches in poor neighborhoods so they wouldn't have to loan money in those neighborhoods and (2) lending institutions concluded that when they did make loans to low and moderate-income families they needed to charge higher rates to compensate for a higher default rate. Between 1980-82, Congress responded to the problem when it passed two additional laws that allowed lending institutions to be compensated for their higher default rate. These laws, the **third and fourth Congressional Legislative Acts** laid the foundation for financial institutions to develop subprime lending and "predatory lending" practices.

The higher rate structure came about under the **third Congressional Legislative Act** which was approved in1980 by another Democratic Congress and signed into law by President Jimmy Carter. The law was called **The Depository Institutions Deregulatory and Monetary Control**

Act (DIDMCA). The DIDMCA eliminated restrictions on interest rates for loans including home loans and allowed lending institutions and credit card companies to charge higher rates to low and moderate-income families to compensate lenders for a higher default rate. In an interview with President Carter on November 16, 1990, (at Hofstra University at a conference on President Carter's Presidency) the President said he agreed to the higher rates because he felt people wouldn't borrow as much money and would manage their debt better because of the higher rates. The second law which completed the process for subprime and "predatory lending" practices was the **fourth of the Congressional Legislative Acts** and passed in 1982, by another Democratic Congress. The CL act was called the **Alternative Mortgage Transaction Parity Act** (AMTPA). The legislation was signed into law by Republican President Ronald Reagan.

The AMTPA created a financial virus called "predatory lending" which allowed lenders to qualify people with low incomes for home ownership. Besides qualifying low-income buyers, the AMTP also allowed lending institutions to qualify people who wanted to refinance their existing homes but who would not have the income to qualify for a larger loan payment. This was accomplished by allowing lending institutions to originate mortgages with features such as adjustable-rate mortgages, negative amortization, charge variable interest rates and use balloon payments. This was significant because it completes the tools needed by lending institutions to establish "predatory lending" practices. It was companies like New Century Financial Corp, a leading subprime mortgage lender, and Countrywide who used the predatory lending tools to take advantage of customers who couldn't understand the financial consequences or had little or no knowledge about financial matters.

Predatory lending generally refers to unethical practices conducted by lending institutions targeting those who are subprime borrowers that lack the sterling credentials needed to qualify for prime loans and the knowledge to understand the lending process. Not all subprime loans were involved in predatory lending. At the same time the virus led to the development of the rise of a new independent mortgage industry, with companies like Countrywide and New Century Financial Corp. who competed against traditional banks and the GSEs. The CRAs required financial institutions to target the "under-served" population which in large part fell on minority groups in low-income areas. These laws created the beginning of a slippery slope of irresponsible financial practices while attempting to social engineer the U.S. housing market. This attempt led to a virus of financial irresponsibility which spread throughout the entire U.S. and world economies. The virus started when the "under-served- or poor populations" were qualified for mortgages with the use of "predatory lending" and subprime practices which were made possible under the AMTPA. The new lending practices ignored traditional lending practices that had been established for a century. Once the subprime and "predatory lending" markets were established these new financial standards and the accompanying attitude spread like a virus throughout the general housing market. The spread of this viral attitude of anything goes was aided by the development of new economic tools (which will be defined later) like MBSs, ABSs, CDs and CDOs or CDSs.

These predatory lending practices allowed introductory interest rates to be lower than normal which allowed three things to happen: **(1)** more of the "under-served or poor populations" qualified for loans, **(2)** home owners who wanted to refinance their homes after their home's value went up dramatically could now qualify for a larger mortgages and **(3)** with the low introductory payment the financial impact for the new home owners or the people who refinanced their homes and used the money to buy other goods and services would be postponed until a later date. The later date would come after: the lending institutions had pooled and sold the mortgages as mortgage-backed securities (MBS) to investors on the open market. The irony is that it was a Democratic controlled Congress that created the tools for "predatory lending" and forced lending institutions to make loans to people who couldn't understand the complexities of the loans they were getting and who also couldn't afford to pay for them.

Many of these same people (mostly Democrats) now blame the Bush administration, the Republican Party and their deregulation policy for the financial crisis. Although it must be pointed out that the deregulation policy did help lead to the Financial Crisis and three Republican Presidents (Ford, Reagan, and Bush 41) did sign some of the 1975-2004 Congressional Legislation acts into law.

The **fifth piece of legislation** came about under the **Tax Reform Act** of 1986 (TRA). The TRA laid the foundation for homeowners to begin using their homes as an ATM account. The TRA of 86 ended interest deductions on consumer loans, such as credit cards and auto loans, but allowed homeowners to deduct interest paid on mortgages. This tax benefit allowed homeowners to reduce their gross income by the cost of mortgage interest paid for a primary residence. For example, a homeowner with income of $50,000 in 1996 who paid $10,000 in interest on his home mortgage would now only have to pay taxes on $40,000 because of his interest deduction. On the other hand, a renter with income of $50,000 and $10,000 in rental expenses would still have to pay taxes on the full $50,000 of income. The net effect of the TRA of 86 was to: (1) encourage more people to buy homes thus driving up the demand and price for homes, and (2) encourage homeowners to become financially irresponsible by taking out home equity loans to pay off consumer debt. Cash from home equity loans encouraged by the 1986 TRA made homeownership/refinancing appear to be the logical solution to solving individual consumer debt problems. Household debt, according to the Federal Reserve, would grow from about $1.4 trillion by year end 1986 to $7.4 trillion by year end 2000, and would finally peak at $12.68 trillion in midyear 2008.

Historically the time period during the early 1980's and continuing until the Financial Crisis of 2007-2008 is referred to as a "culture of consumption" and a "culture of financial irresponsibility" (an attitude that anything goes). During this period credit cards became easier to obtain as financial institutions aggressively chased new accounts as consumers were willing to load up their balance sheets with large amounts of debt. According to the Federal Reserve statistics, during the ten-year period from December 1986 to July 1996, "revolving credit," including credit card debt, had risen from $136 to $454 billion.

The **sixth of Congressional Legislative Acts** in its attempt to reform the banking industry with the **1989 Financial Institutions Reform Recovery and Enforcement Act (FIRREA).** The Act now required the appropriate Federal regulatory agency to prepare a public written evaluation after completing an examination of an institution's record in meeting the credit needs of its entire community, including any low-and moderate-income neighborhoods. FIRREA established a four-tiered CRA rating of banks in order to **force** social engineering lending practices upon financial institutions so they would have to comply with providing loans to small business and **credit to the "under-served or poor populations."** The four-tiered CRA rating system had performance levels of 'Outstanding', 'Satisfactory', 'Needs to Improve', or 'Substantial Noncompliance'. FIRREA with its four-tiered CRA rating system greatly increased the ability of advocacy groups, researchers, and other analysts to perform more-sophisticated, quantitative analyses of banks records. This in turn allowed these advocacy groups to **influence the lending policies of the banks to meet the advocacy groups' ever-increasing demands for lesser loan requirements and more loans.**

As mentioned, this **social engineering** process of making financially unqualified individuals homeowners begins with the HMDA in 1975, the CRA of 1977 and the expansion of its requirements under different Congressional acts, such as the AMTPA of 1982 and the TRA in 1986 during the Reagan years. A 1992 study by the Boston Fed concluded that mortgage-lending discrimination was systemic. The Boston Fed produced a manual for mortgage lenders (that was supported by the entire Federal Reserve Board) stating: "discrimination may be observed when a lender's underwriting policies contain arbitrary or outdated criteria that effectively disqualify many urban or lower-income minority applicants." **Some of these "outdated" criteria included: (1) the size of the mortgage payment relative to income, (2) credit history, (3) savings history and (4) income verification.** The Boston Fed model produced a justification for financial institutions like Countrywide to develop predatory lending practices. The Boston Fed study ruled that participation in a credit-counseling program should be taken as evidence of an applicant's ability to manage debt. # 3

In 1992, a Democratic Congress passed the **seventh of the Congressional Legislative Acts; the Housing and Community Development Act (HCDA]**. The Act was signed into law by Republican President George H. W. Bush, (but only after he raised serious concerns about some provisions of the way the bill targeted assistance to expanding homeownership). The Act amended the charter of Fannie Mae and Freddie Mac the Government Sponsored Enterprises (GSEs) **to reflect Congress's view that the GSEs "have an affirmative obligation to facilitate the financing of affordable housing for low-income and moderate-income families."** # 4 **For the first time, the GSEs were required to meet affordable housing goals set annually by the Department of Housing and Urban Development (HUD) and approved by Congress.** As mentioned, the initial annual goal for low-income and moderate-income mortgage purchases for each GSE was 30% of the total number of dwelling units financed by mortgage purchases. The goal was increased to 55% by 2007.

The Clinton Administration in 1993 passed the **eighth of the Congressional Legislative Acts** in an attempt to reform the 1977 CRA. The goal was to make CRA examinations more consistent, to better clarify performance standards, and reduce cost and compliance burdens. This new legislation entitled Community Reinvestment Reform Act of 1993 was the eighth of the Congressional Legislative Acts. The Act ordered new regulations for the CRA which would increase the availability for mortgages for inner cities, and distressed rural communities. Some of the key regulations in the Act are as follows:

(Section 101) "Amends the Community Reinvestment Act of 1977 to direct the appropriate Federal financial supervisory agencies to jointly develop a format for collecting data from regulated financial institutions in connection with examinations of their record of meeting the credit needs of their local communities, including low-and moderate-income neighborhoods."

(Section 102) "Prescribes guidelines under which the appropriate Federal financial supervisory agencies, as part of their written evaluations of the institutions under their purview, must actively solicit comments from affected community members, with particular emphasis upon low- and moderate-income and minority residents."

(Section 104) Amends the CRA to require financial institutions to be rated on the adequacy of their record of meeting community credit needs. **Precludes such institutions from receiving a rating unless they have extended significant amounts of credit in low-income neighborhoods**, and not merely been in compliance with a plan for extending such credit in the future.

As a result of the above legislation, community groups like ACORN (the Association of Community Organization for Reform Now which is an international collection of autonomous community-based organization that advocates for low-and moderate-income families) or the Boston-based Neighborhood Assistance Corporation of America were able to pressure American's lending institutions into making a flood of subprime loans to consumers who were not credit worthy**.** In his **New York Post article "The Real Scandal" Stan Liebowitz** noted how Chase Manhattan and J.P, Morgan donated hundreds of thousands of dollars to ACORN around the same time they were to apply for permission to merge and needed to comply with CRA regulations. Liebowitz additionally states in his article: How the Federal Government "invited the mortgage mess" in which he states how Fannie Mae singled out Countrywide Financial as a "paragon" of nondiscriminatory lending who works with community activists, following "the most flexible underwriting criteria permitted." # 5

In a September 23, 2008, statement to CNN by Congressman Ron Paul who sat on the U. S. House Committee on Financial Services partially attributed the ongoing subprime mortgage crisis to the CRA charging it with "… forcing banks to lend to people who normally would be rejected as bad credit risks."

A common belief is that it was the banks that came up with the idea of looser underwriting standards on their own, while regulators were just asleep on the job. The truth was that regulators relaxed lending standards at the behest of community groups like ACORN Housing, and Boston-based Neighborhood Assistance Corporation of America.

The new rules created under the Community Reinvestment Reform Act of 1993 went into effect on January 31, 1995. These new rules required banks under "Section 104" to get a numerical assessment on the number of loans made to the "under-served populations" to get a satisfactory CRA rating. The numerical assessments were the government's attempt to **social engineer a broader based home ownership by using home-loan data broken down by neighborhood, income group, and race. Community groups such as ACORN Housing, Boston-based Neighborhood Assistance Corporation of America and the New Jersey Citizen Action-led coalition were encouraged under "Section 102" to complain when banks were not loaning enough to specified neighborhoods or under-served populations.** It was also pointed out by the Senate Banking Committee that these community groups received an estimated $9.5 billion in services and salaries by 2000 as a result of CRA. The legislation was successful in that the number of CRA subprime mortgage loans increased by 39 percent between 1993 and 1998 while regular loans increased by only 17 percent.

Adding to and supporting the "culture of financial irresponsibility" was an ideology of laissez-faire economics that was reflective in the **ninth of the Congressional Legislative Acts** under the **Gramm-Leach-Bliley Act (GLBA)** of 1999. The key to the passage of both the GLBA and the **Commodity Futures Modernization Act** CFMA of 2000 (which would be the **tenth of the Congressional Legislation acts**) was the leadership of Republican Senator Phil Gramm. Gramm was on the Senate banking committee and was one of the most effective proponents of this free market/laissez-faire philosophy. With his force of personality, he pushed through laws and promoted policies which would be supported by both Democrats and Republicans that would lead to the deregulation of financial markets. In 1999, the first of two key laws pushed through Congress by Senator Gramm was the Gramm-Leach-Bliley Act (GLBA). The GLBA of 1999, was the most significant financial services legislation since the Great Depression. The GLBA was true to Gramm's beliefs as it reflected a free-market philosophy when it allowed creation of financial supermarkets. This was accomplished by a policy that allowed the commercial banks, securities firms and insurers to offer an array of financial services between themselves with no oversight. This policy had never been allowed before. By allowing for this creation of the supermarket atmosphere the GLBA capped the government's oversight abilities of Wall Street and knocked down Depression-era barriers that restricted the expansion, development and reach of financial institutions. The GLBA accomplished this supermarket effect by removing barriers between commercial and investment banks that had been instituted to reduce the risk of financial economic catastrophes while at the same time it split up oversight of the conglomerates among government agencies. **Consequently, there was no person or agency looking at how the various financial institutions would interact with one another or what effect their individual actions would have on the financial wellbeing of society.** Finally, the legislation ensured that there would be virtually no regulation of the complex financial instruments known as derivatives (the new financial tool which will be defined below as a key tool for the new global frontier) or the institutions like AIG and Lehman Brothers that sold them. # 6

After the passage of the Gramm-Leach-Bliley Act, Gramm with the support of senior Clinton administration officials and Congress pushed through the **tenth of the Congressional Legislative acts** with the **Commodity Futures Modernization Act** (CFMA) of December 2000. Support for the CFMA included Clinton's Treasury Secretary Lawrence Summers, Arthur Levitt Jr., head of the Securities and Exchange Commission and Alan Greenspan, chairman of the Federal Reserve Board. The bi-partisan group argued that too many restrictions on credit derivatives would hurt financial markets within the United States and encourage traders to take their business overseas. At the time of its passage the CFMA had the support of lawmakers of both parties (passed as part of a larger bill by unanimous consent) and the Clinton Administration. Although some critics argued the lack of oversight would allow for the development of abuses that could threaten the economy, and the conservative ideology of deregulation which was the value of the day. # 7 Later, six Democrats on the ten member America's Financial Crisis Inquiry Commission "The Commission" which was created to investigate the Financial Crisis concluded that---the net effect of these two laws which supported the ideology of deregulation, had allowed Wall Street to run wild. The Commission concluded that the ideology of deregulation along with the financial industry's greed and sloppy risk management lead to the Financial Crisis.

It was a combination of the virus of financial irresponsibility and the public appetite for consumption that created the foundation for the "perfect financial storm" that led to the Financial Crisis. With Congress, HUD, the GSE's pushing financial institutions to continue to make more subprime loans an **open-door policy based on financial irresponsibility** was created for **Wall Street.** Wall Street's financial irresponsibility was centered around three events: (1) financial institutions were required to make more loans to the "under-served population", (2) new economic tools were created and adopted by financial institutions, and (3) the open-door policy for Wall Street came about as the rating agencies, with their inadequate and irresponsible evaluations of the new economic tools or financial instruments were the key players in spreading the **virus of financial irresponsibility.**

Lehman Brothers is an example of the practice of financial irresponsibility brought about by Wall Street and the rating agencies' open-door policies. Lehman was one of the first Wall Street firms to move into the business of mortgage origination and made loans to the under-served population. In 1977, Lehman purchased Colorado-based lender Aurora Loan Services and in 2000 they expanded to the West Coast and purchased subprime mortgage lender BNC Mortgage LLC. Lehman quickly became a force in the subprime market. By 2003 Lehman made $18.2 billion in loans and ranked third in lending. By 2004, they topped $40 billion for the year. By 2006, Aurora and BNC were lending almost $50 billion per month. Lehman had morphed into a real estate hedge fund disguised as an investment bank. By 2008, Lehman had assets of $639 billion supported by only $22.5 billion of capital. In such a highly leveraged structure, a 3-5 percent decline in real estate values would wipe out all their capital. The decline of mortgage values in 2008 forced Lehman into bankruptcy on September 15, 2008.

The public's appetite for consumption can be explained and even justified by some as the key to a growing economy. It is estimated that about 70% of the US economy is tied to consumer spending. High levels of consumption promote economic growth, but it can also lead to personal financial instability as a result of financial irresponsibility. This is especially true when consumption is fueled by asset appreciation and low levels of personal savings as was experienced during the period of the "culture of consumption." The passage of the CRA and its supporting legislation combined with the development of the financial virus led to the development and spread of the housing virus and a huge demand for new homes. As the markets for new homes were created and more people could now buy a new home the viruses had created an upward pressure on housing prices which led to people using their newfound wealth (more equity in their homes) to enjoy their life more and consume more. The key question is what affect or how much did the CRA and its loan policies contribute to the 2008 Financial Crisis? Opinions are mixed.

The Financial Crisis Inquiry Commission "The Commission" formed by the US Congress in 2009 to investigate the causes of the 2007-2008 financial crisis concluded "the CRA was not a significant factor in subprime lending or the crisis." #8 Ben Bernanke, then Chairman of the Federal Reserve, wrote that experience and research contradict "the charge that CRA was at the root of, or otherwise contributed in any substantive way to, the current mortgage difficulties." #9 A third opinion from former Chair of the Federal Reserve, Janet Yellen, was: "... independent mortgage companies made risky 'higher-priced' loans at more than twice the rate of the banks and thrifts: most CRA loans were responsibly made and were not the 'higher-priced' loans that have contributed to the current crisis." #10

As "The Commission", Ben Bernanke, and Janet Yellen, have all pointed out the financial crisis was greater than the collapse of the subprime-mortgage market. The credit excess that created the financial crisis was global. There were many bubbles, and they extended beyond housing in many countries to commercial real estate mortgages and loans, to credit cards, auto loans, and student loans. Bernanke and Yellen also pointed out that there were financial bubbles for the securitized products that converted loans and mortgages into complex toxic and destructive financial instruments. These investments were then made available to local governments, hedge funds, industrial loans, and corporate bonds.

Given the magnitude of the above opinions one could safely say that the Community Reinvestment Act of 1977 & 1993 (CRA's) were not directly responsible for the 2007-2008 Financial Crisis. However, the CRAs can be labeled as partly and indirectly responsible. As mentioned, the social engineering philosophy embedded in the CRA was reinforced in numerous legislative acts that did contribute directly to the financial crisis. The combination of the legislative acts and HUD's action between 1975-2007 created a slippery slope of a "culture of financial irresponsibility." In November 2000 Fannie Mae announced that the Department of Housing and Urban Development (HUD) would soon require it to dedicate 55% of its business to low and moderate-income families. In 2001 Fannie Mae announced that it had acquired $10 billion in specially targeted CRA loans more than one and a half years ahead of schedule and announced its goal to finance over $500 billion in CRA loans by 2010, about one third of loans anticipated to be financed by Fannie Mae during that period. An example of the "culture of financial irresponsibility" the CRAs created can be seen with Countrywide. In October 2013, a federal jury found Countrywide (who had become the nation's largest mortgage lenders) guilty of defrauding federal mortgage giants Fannie Mae and Freddie Mac of $848 million on loans they bought from Countrywide before the B of A takeover in 2008. The B of A takeover was for 4 billion dollars in stock—a sixth of the amount of its market value before the crisis began. In 1992, Countrywide began its program of nondiscriminatory lending with a $1 billion commitment to low-income loans which had grown to $80 billion by 1999 and $600 billion by early 2003.

As the public and private mortgage markets expanded, competition played a key role in lending practices being lowered. Incentives to screen less on loan applications by regulators and the pressure on financial institutions to maintain market share were key factors leading to predatory lending practices and the mortgage default crisis. It must also be remembered that another key factor was pressure from Community groups such as ACORN Housing, Boston-based Neighborhood Assistance Corporation of America and the New Jersey Citizen Action-led coalition. These Community groups were encouraged by the CRAs to complain when banks were not loaning enough to specified neighborhoods or under-served populations. In order to deal with these pressures and keep market their share Countrywide which was one of the nation's largest and most aggressive mortgage brokers, developed a loan program in 2007 called HSSL (High Speed Swim Lane). HSSL was a great example of predatory lending as the program stripped back underwriter reviews for loans, leaving few to no controls in the loan approval process. It was even claimed that the borrower's income wasn't independently verified by Countrywide and went unreviewed by underwriters. While Countrywide employees described HSSL loans as "loser loans", (according to testimony given in their bankruptcy trail) at the same time, Countrywide had assured the GSEs that underwriting standards had been tightened. # 11

Lending practices by independent mortgage companies like Countrywide and New Century Financial Corp were obvious factors contributing to the Financial Crisis. Just like the CRA requirements and the legislation that followed were also major factors. But the regulators in charge of enforcing the CRA requirements also had a major role to play. The regulators even told banks that much higher LTV's (loan to value) were an appropriate way to meet the CRA obligations and also praised the banks for the lowering and or the elimination of down payments. The regulators also instructed banks to consider alternatives to traditional credit histories because CRA targeted borrowers often lacked traditional credit histories. **Banks were not only expected to become creative with their lending standards, but were told that lending standards that exceeded that of regulators would be considered evidence of unfair lending.** What happened to the **"clean hands doctrine"?** There are some great inconsistencies between the regulators and the CRAs. For example, the 1977 CRA did not require institutions to make high-risk loans that may bring losses to the institutions, but stated the loans should be: "consistent with the safe and sound operation of such institutions". However, a Treasury Department study published in 2000 found that the CRAs had successfully gotten financial institutions to lower down payments not just for CRA loans, but for all mortgages. # 12

History has shown that you can pass all the laws and create all the regulation you want, but if you don't enforce the laws because: (1) you have the wrong people overseeing the regulatory institutions, or (2) society as a whole has adopted an ideology that allows society's passions to get out of control and exercise little or no constraint, then the laws or regulatory institutions have little or no effect. The Sherman Antitrust Act of 1890 demonstrates this point. As a result of widespread agitation with the practice of big business like Standard Oil during the late 1880's, Congress enacted the Sherman Antitrust Act.

The act was signed into law by President Benjamin Harrison on July 2, 1890. It stated: "Every contract, combination in the form of a trust or otherwise, or conspiracy, in restraint of trade or commerce among the several states, or with foreign nations is hereby declared to be illegal…." Because Congress failed to provide definitions of the terms "trust," "conspiracy," and "monopoly," it left to the courts the task of interpreting and applying their own definition. The result was ineffective regulation of trust and monopolies even though the law appeared to be quite comprehensive.

The ineffectiveness of the act is exemplified in the 1895 case of the U.S. vs. E.C. Knight & Co., (156 U.S. 1) in which the U.S. Supreme Court held that the mere control of 98 percent of the sugar refining business of the country did not in itself constitute an act in restraint of trade. Under the Knight decision, any action against manufacturing monopolies would need to be taken by individual states, making such regulation extremely difficult with regards to out-of-state monopolies because states are prohibited from discriminating against out-of-state goods by, among other things, the Dormant Commerce Clause and Article I section 10 of the U.S. Constitution. The responsibility for the failure of the Sherman Antitrust Act should not be charged exclusively to the judiciary. The legislature failed to amend the act, the executive branch failed to enforce it because the economic and social philosophy of society was based on a laissez-faire philosophy which led to the regulatory agencies as well as the courts to evaluate the activities of corporate society accordingly. During this time period (1870's - 1902) something over 5,000 industrial establishments were consolidated into about 300 trusts or corporations, and of these 198 were formed in the period from 1898 to 1902. (In theory, the Sherman Antitrust Act passed in 1890 made all of the trusts' consolidation illegal.)

Historically society's values change slowly as they move in one direction until they have reached a climax or a crisis point as a result of a conflict of social and economic forces within society. After the crisis society tends to move into a corrective mode which leads to new values or new institutions or agencies that have influence over society. Such was the case with the Progressive Movement and the New Deal. It wasn't until the Progressive Movement and the leadership of Teddy Roosevelt and Woodrow Wilson that the social philosophy of the country changed and the Sherman Antitrust Act was enforced.

What all of this means is that there is a time within history when society adopts **ideologies** that allow its passions to get out of control. This applied to the ideologies of both the Democrats and Republicans as it is applied to the events leading up to the 2007-08 Financial Crisis.

On the Republican side legislation was passed which encouraged homeowners to use their homes like ATM machines and pile-up large debts. The Republican ideology of the best government is the one that governs the least contributed to the country's financial problems. As mentioned, during this period of rapid growth no one agency or groups of agencies were permitted to evaluate and monitor the activities of mortgage lenders, Wall Street or the new financial instruments that were being created. To make matters worse, the Securities and Exchange Commission (SEC) in October 2004 relaxed the net capital requirements for five investment banks—Goldman Sachs, Merrill Lynch, Lehman Brothers, Bear Stearns, and Morgan Stanley. This new policy freed these financial institutions to leverage their initial investments by up to 30 or 40 times. Within four years three of the five banks were no longer in existence—they either went out of business or were absorbed by other banks.

This Republican ideology developed during the formative years (1600's up to the mid 1800's) of our country's economy. The marketplace consisted of local or regional (the Southern economy v. the Northern economy) markets and thus little to no government regulation was necessary. But in the period following the Civil War and with the construction of the transcontinental railroads the marketplace changed and began to move from a local and regional marketplace to a national market. With this change came social, economic and thus political stress within society. The old environment pitted man against nature in man's quest to advance his economic and thus social status while the new environment pitted man against man in his quest to advance. This new environmental competition was led by such greats as John D. Rockefeller and Andrew Carnegie who were leaders in creating the new industrial society. One of the results of this new industrial society was the creation of greater economic inequalities as new economic tools and new business practices were created such as trusts and holding companies. The problem with these **new tools was that society never anticipated their creation and thus had no laws to regulate them. The same is true about the new tools that created the Financial Crisis.** In both cases during the landed frontier and the global frontier the new tools allowed for the development of abusive practices within society which eventually led to new laws to try and control them. This same pattern developed in the 1990's and into the early 21st century with the construction and development of the international markets. At this point with the development of globalization, we as a nation have begun to move away from our dependence on our national market and began to become more and more dependent upon the global markets. As the global markets for the new frontier developed numerous businesses and different financial institutions **developed new tools such as hedge funds, CDOs and CDSs in order to take advantage of the new frontier**. Just as in the late 1800's and early 1900's new tools were created in the 1990's and the early 21st century that society had never thought of and, therefore, there was no regulatory legislation put in place to control the actions of the new business elite or their new practices. Because the economic growth during these periods was first looked upon as positive there was little clamor for government regulation from any of the social or economic classes. However, as time passed, social and economic differences seemed to become more permanent during both the old frontier of the late 19th century and the new frontier of the early 21st century. The result was during both periods a movement developed which wanted and required more government control in order to deal with the economic and social stress that had developed between the classes. But it was the Panic of 1907 and the Financial Crisis of 2007-2008 that made the societies of both periods finally realize that new changes in society had developed and required new types of government regulations which imposed new responsibilities on the Federal Government. In both cases critics tried to blame the government for not correcting the problems before they developed and for not having the wisdom to see the consequences before they happened—in each case hindsight is 20-20. In many cases it's only after you travel the path that your choices become clear. It is a lot easier to criticize leaders for not dealing with the problems (of the newly created holding companies or trusts of the late 1800's or early 1900's as well as the hedge funds of the 21st century) after the problems have occurred than before they materialized.

As stated, it was this free-market/laissez-faire philosophy that evolved out of America's colonial experience and America's experiences in the early to mid-1800's that transformed this country from a land frontier or agricultural society to the greatest industrial power in the world by the 1890's. However, as the "creative destruction" **(refers to the economic structure of a country being revolutionized from within which leads to the destruction of the old values, practices and the structure of society and the creation of a new values, practices and the restructuring of society)** of America's agricultural society took place it was replaced by a new industrialized society with the same free market/ laissez-faire philosophy. The old free market/laissez values needed to be modified in the new complex industrialized society in order to adjust the impact the new industrialization had on individuals within society. This modification in values and thus institutions was first introduced on a wide scale in the early 1900's by the Progressive Movement and reached its completion as a result of the Great Depression of the 1930's in the New Deal. The New Deal was a major watershed in American History. One of the most important results of the New Deal was the creation of a new role for the Federal Government. From the New Deal forward, the American people expected the Federal Government to be responsible for stabilizing the economy. Consequently, if Bush was going to do the right thing for good governance, he had no choice but to develop his "all-in policy." After the New Deal, like with Bush's "all-in policy", everyone agreed the government had to assume a bigger role, but not everyone agreed as to what that role should be. In general, the Democrats developed more of an attitude that the government should be protective against the harsher elements within society, while the Republicans developed the idea that the government should provide a stable environment so that the individual could develop his/her own potential. The Republicans also saw too much government intervention as a violation of the basic values the country was founded upon and government intervention was seen as a restriction upon the individual and his/her ability to advance him or herself within society. However, changes in government behavior were and are going to be needed, because of globalization. Changes that developed as a result of this new world economy had made the world's countries more interdependent upon each other. As the forces of "creative destruction" worked their magic on old world institutions that began changing the world from independent national economies to interdependent world economies, leaders in the United States and the world failed to recognize the transformation. Even though there was the development of new economic tools such as credit derivatives and credit default swaps that were being used in a new globalized world economy, political and financial leaders alike continued to hang onto the old views and value system of a nationalist economy.

As the United States and the World moved into a new economic frontier called globalization, much like the transformation from the landed frontier to the industrial frontier, the globalized frontier provided many new opportunities with the use of new financial tools called derivatives which will be discussed later. As with the "creative destruction" that took place from our earlier transformation into an industrial society, there would be new economic tools such as derivatives being created by the new and larger financial service industry that aided the development of "creative destruction" of our society into a globalized society. Historically, as with all new economic tools, society at the time, did not understand nor recognize the consequential impact these new economic tools would have. Globalization coupled with the use of derivatives were two of the major factors that led to the Financial Crisis of 2007-2008. As with this earlier transformation into an industrial society, where the role of government was changed as a result of the new economic tools like trusts and holding companies the role of government in the new globalized society needs to change and is in the process of changing, hence there will be another fundamental ideological shift—just how much of a shift only history will tell. At a meeting President Bush held at Camp David in October 2008, he indicated a shift was necessary when he stated: "Given that the world has never been more interconnected, it is essential that we work together because we're in this crisis together."

As a follow-up to President Bush's comments, at a conference at the London School of Economics, in January 2009, Fed Chairman Ben Bernanke gave a speech entitled: The Crisis and the Policy Response, in which he stated: "Finally, a clear lesson of the recent period is that the world is too interconnected for nations to go it alone in their economic, financial, and regulatory policies. International cooperation is thus essential if we are to address the crisis successfully and provide the basis for a healthy, sustained recovery." # 13

A possible early indication of change that could take place occurred October 15, 2008, when British Prime Minister Gordon Brown called for global talks aimed at creating better international rules to guide financial markets. In part, the international summit that was held on the financial crisis turned into a debate over the future shape of capitalism. At the October Camp David meeting, French President Sarkozy and President Barroso of the European Commission called for the building of a new financial order and a new system of global capitalism. (The White House press release October 18,2008) President Sarkozy denounced the failures in the US system that had led to the global crisis. President Sarkozy also stated that it is **"necessary to rebuild the entire global financial and monetary system from the bottom up."** Of course, President George W Bush preferred the current model of national regulation. Globalization could be leading to the "creative destruction" process by creating an environment where national regulation will eventually **in the long run** give way to more international regulation. The summit ended with President Bush, French President Nicolas Sarkozy—then the current head of the European Union—and the current head of the European Commission President Jose' Manuel Barrosos agreeing to put together a series of summits to address the long-term challenges of globalization**. President Sarkozy stated the goal of the future summits was to "build together a capitalism of the future."** #14 It appears that the European leaders in their October 2008 summit were suggesting changes to international rules to guide financial markets---although there was a lot of **rhetoric,** no changes were made. This **rhetoric** could be the first step in the "creative destruction" of national markets.

President Bush's response to these leaders and their goal of a new international regulatory system was expressed before the G 20 conference in November of 2008. He stated that he would resist calls to impose regulations he sees as too strict. "The crisis was not a failure of the free market system. And the answer is not to try to reinvent that system."

The European leaders who were thinking of "**build together a capitalism of the future"** found it to be more difficult than they anticipated. This was demonstrated by the problems experienced by the European Union and the profound impacts that five countries (Portugal, Italy, Ireland, Greece, and Spain = PIIGS) had on the rest of Europe during the European debt crisis of 2009-10. Consequently, these five countries were referred to as PIIGS because their excessive spending habits and irresponsible decisions led to unsustainable national debt levels and weaker economies, relative to other nations in the European Union. The PIIGS demonstrated the problems of one organization trying to regulate the economies of a group of nations.

In 1999, European Union members began to issue and utilize the same currency—the Euro. As a result of this event, debts issued by the individual members of the union began to be merged. Initially, these developments seemed to be a positive occurrence as it was thought the economic risk could be spread amongst the EU members. However, as time went on, it was evident that some countries (the PIIGS) were more financially irresponsible as they began to accumulate excessive debt.

Another example of one organization trying to coordinate international economies was exemplified by Greece in October 2009. In that year Greece declared that they had been underreporting their countries deficit numbers for several years. The announcement had an adverse effect on the nation's financial systems as investors worried about Greece's ability to repay its debt. Greece was not the only country in the European Union to experience financial worries as the rest of the PIIGS also had high sovereign debt.

The problem was the PIIGS's financial behavior made investors wary of investing in the EU. When the Financial Crisis of 2007-08 became a global crisis, pressure began to mount on central banks worldwide. This was especially true for the European Union. The European Central Bank acted quickly, helping to solve the problem by implementing policies that were favorable for their economies, such as: lowering interest rates, even to negative territory, and implementing quantitative easing [QE] programs.

The PIIGS were saved when a variety of relief packages starting in May 2010 were introduced by the EU. In May 2010, Greece received a bailout package to keep it from defaulting on its debt. Ireland similarly received a relief package in November. In May 2011, Portugal became the next nation to receive a bailout. Shortly thereafter, the European Central bank began buying bonds from Italy and Spain to provide them with more liquidity to support their financial institutions.

It appears a process that could lead to "creative destruction" was being formulated in the minds of some EU leaders as they talked about building a capitalism of the future together as the Financial Crisis had exposed the weakness of the old order of national regulations of financial markets. EU leaders as expressed by their rhetoric appear to be moving into a direction of creating a new international regulatory system.

As of 2024 that new international regulatory system had not been created. If and when a new system is created it would most likely not be a revolutionary process, but an evolutionary process like all major value changes that history has produced. It should be clear that the author is not advocating the development of an international regulatory system, but if one were to develop, it would be over many years or even decades.

Possible examples of this evolutionary change could be beginning to emerge with the development of digital currencies and digital IDs. On June 28, 2023, Reuters reported that a total of 130 countries representing 98% of the global economies are now exploring digital versions of **their currencies**, with almost half in advanced development, pilot or launch stages. These countries believe that a digital currency will be an upgrade over traditional forms of money, because it would flow more easily around the world through digital wallets; thus, bypassing the messy web of commercial banks and the money-transfer businesses. Digital currency is a new form of currency that is issued electronically by **each country's central bank (CBDC or central bank digital currency)**. Generally, there are two types of CBDCs: those designed for use by the financial institutions and those for use by the general public. The currency can be used by households and businesses to make payments. If the Federal

Government felt the economy needed stimulus, they could just deposit stimulus checks into U.S. citizen's digital currency accounts. On the other hand, if they felt the economy was running too hot, they could freeze a portion of a citizen's account to reduce consumer spending. There is a hypothetical fear by some that electronic payments make it easier for a state to monitor its citizens actions. No one knows the future but is it possible that over time central banks worldwide will take digital currency one step further by standardizing their CDBC into one world currency in order to make global transactions easier. # 15

At the G20 conference held in India in September of 2023, there appeared that a consensus had been reached on the issue of digital identification and digital currency. As a result of the G20 meeting a comprehensive document was produced titled "G20 Policy Recommendations for Advancing Financial Inclusion and Productivity Gains Through Digital Public Infrastructure".

The document highlighted the potential of digital IDs to foster financial inclusion, particularly in low-and middle-income countries where a lack of proper documentation often serves as a formidable barrier to access financial services. The concept of a digital Id was just one facet of a broader recommendation known as "Digital Public Infrastructure." This broad term includes not only digital IDs, but digital payments, and data exchanges within the financial sector of these countries. # 16

An historical example of this currency and economic transformation process occurred shortly after the American War for Independence. Before the war there were 13 independent provinces which held loyalties to England. After the War there were 13 independent states: each with their own currency as well as a tariff system to protect their own economies. Because these trading barriers and the multiple currencies created economic barriers that hindered economic growth the newly established states decided to eliminate the trade barriers and create a uniform currency.

Another example of this same process, as mentioned, took place in Europe in 1999 when the European Union members began to issue and utilize the same currency---the Euro. In world history there are many examples of this process. There are also anti-globalization groups who believe that international agreements and global financial institutions, such as the International Monetary Fund (IMF) and the World Trade Organization, undermine local decision-making.

Section: 2

The Creation of New Economic Tools

A prominent economist once said: **"To see economic policy as a problem of choice between rival ideologies is the greatest error of our time."** # 1 John Kenneth Galbraith explains how the lessons of history create an understanding of human behavior and how societies have ignored the lessons from the past when they themselves are trying to manage the processes that bring about the social and economic changes within their own societies. In discussing the process of managing social and economic change Galbraith explains the development of new **economic tools.** "From history we can also see, more vividly than in any other way, how money and the techniques (economic tools) for its management and mismanagement evolved and how they now serve or fail to serve." # 2

In his book: **Money: Whence it Came, Where It Went**, Galbraith points out how people too often view changing social and economic activities or events from a particular ideology, but he rejects ideological preferences and instead shows the recurring economic patterns that lead to the development of the lessons of history.

The history of the United States shows how the shifting of positions in ideology demonstrates how ideologies themselves are only one tool for better understanding developing economic events and the historical imperatives or lessons they create. In the United States, during the

Presidency of Ronald Reagan, Milton Friedman's free-market ideas and its supporting ideology of limited government intervention were popular and seemed to provide the correct insight into understanding society's economic needs. At the same time, Galbraith ideas of deficit spending to avoid depression and government stabilization were not viewed as useful. But in recent years, as a result of the Financial Crisis of 2007-2008, the wisdom of Galbraith's ideas was recognized by both Democrats and Republicans alike. The change came in October of 2008 when Henry Paulson and Ben Bernanke marched into the Oval Office and convinced President Bush that the financial crisis was so severe the government had no choice but to intervene decisively with large sums of tax-payer's dollars (Troubled Asset Relief Program) to rescue private markets. Hence, the free-market philosophy of Milton Friedman was out. The lesson is that there is no single theory or ideology that can be used to understand and or control the production, development and management of material wealth in any society. Galbraith once said: "I'm in favor of privatization, or I'm deeply in favor of public ownership. I'm in favor of whatever works in the particular case...." # 3

In **Money** the lessons of history are replayed again and again as Galbraith discusses the economies of various regions of the world and time periods to explain how different forms of money from metal coins to commercial paper were created. In his history of the banking system, he explains the development of commercial paper, the centralized banking system in Great Britain and the subsequent development of the Federal Reserve System in the United States. He also describes how the **cycles of euphoria and panic** are repeated as the lessons of history are ignored as each new generation feels it has developed the Midas touch and that this time it will be different. The length of the cycle "...came to accord roughly with the time it took people to forget the last disaster." # 4 Galbraith points out how the cycles of euphoria and disaster have reoccurred over the past two hundred and fifty years starting from the time of John Law's founding of a land bank in France in 1716 and its subsequent demise in 1720 and ending with Bernard Cornfield and his Equity Funding Corporation of America in 1973.

Historically in the United States, speculation which led to the cycles of euphoria in the early 19th century was a local phenomenon with little or no national impact,but as society developed with its new technologies speculation became a national phenomenon in the late 19th and early 20th century. This new economic euphoria in a new emerging national economy eventually led to great economic and social imbalances and abuses within society. These imbalances and abuses eventually led to government action under the Progressive Movement and later the New Deal. As the twenty-first century emerged so did the global economy along with the cycle of euphoria which was again introduced by the fever of speculation which in turn produced disaster in the world economy in 2007-2008. Galbraith uses the phrase **"kit of tools"** to describe the historical development of **monetary** and **fiscal policy** as they were applied to control the various cycles of euphoria that emerged between the eighteenth and twenty-first centuries. Economists believed that if mastered, the "kit of tools" could be used to guide the economy. During each step as the "kit of tools" was being developed economic policy makers thought they had tamed the business cycle only later to find that they had not. For **monetary policy** the "kit of tools" includes such things as: (1) the central bank policy or bank rate, (2) open-market operations, (3) the creation of the gold standard, (4) the Federal Reserve System and (5) the Bretton Woods agreements which included the creation of both the International Monetary Fund and what today is called the World Bank Group. These are the tools used to try to stabilize the economy by controlling interest rates and the supply of money. **Fiscal policy** and Keynesian economics use government spending and taxation to influence the economy. The purpose of fiscal policy is to ensure that money is available to be borrowed and would be spent in order to produce economic recovery. Like John Maynard Keynes, Galbraith believed the main role of government was to regulate business cycles.

If Galbraith were alive today, he would add the **derivative markets** which produced the mortgage-backed securities crisis of 2007-2008 to the cycles of euphoria and disaster and the lessons of history. The name derivative comes from the fact that the value of the securities is "derived" from underlying assets like stocks, bonds, commodities, that are bundled into **asset-backed commercial paper** like mortgage-backed securities (MBS). A mortgage-backed security is an asset-backed security whose cash flows are derived from or backed by the principal and interest payments of a set of mortgage loans that have been bundled together. If both the house and the residential mortgage pass-through certificates (MBS) are owned by a United States Government agency (GSE) only the **principal and interest payments** of the MBS are guaranteed for those certificates. The government is NOT guaranteeing the price of the house, stock or bonds. For example, if a private-label or a non-agency investment-banking firm owns a house but sells the credit risk to another party in the form of a Collateralized Debt Obligation (CDO) the value of the house may drop, but the interest payments still pass-through to the owner of the CDO. If the principal and interest payments are not made under a private-label institution then the values of the CDO and the house both decline in value. The use of derivatives on Wall Street is known as hedging (hedging the risk) and during a 6-year period between 2002 and 2008 the complexity of the structure of derivatives as well as their prevalence ballooned from $106 trillion in 2002 to a euphoric $531 trillion in 2008. As a result, **derivatives became a new form of money for the financial industry.**

To simplify this complicated process involving MBSs, credit derivatives and CDOs the following definitions are put forth.

1. MBS-- mortgage back securities (involves pooling and repackaging regular and subprime loans together into bonds or securities and selling the bonds to investors).
2. Creating CDOs—Collateralized Debt Obligations (happens when financial institutions sell the income **[the payment from the note to someone who just wants to invest in the interest rate]** from the MBS ---while still owning the mortgages or bonds). The financial institutions then divide the interest income produced by the MBSs into different credit quality tranches or tiers of risk (CDOs) and then sell that income from the different tiers of risk to investors.

3. These tranches are then rated by a Credit Rating Agency. The ratings were relied upon by investors to evaluate risk.
4. After the CDOs are rated investors then bought a portion of the income stream from the CDO—based on the amount of risk they were willing to take. The higher the risk meant a higher interest rate return and likewise a lower risk meant a lower return.

This "new creation of money" by the derivatives markets led to the housing bubble. What made the derivative markets possible were the actions by the rating agencies, HUD and the Congressional Legislation acts passed between 1975-2007. The derivative markets started to develop after the 2000 dot-com bubble popped and interest rates in the United States and elsewhere were lowered to stimulate the economy. As interest rates declined, people shifted funds into housing. Home values rose, making American homeowners wealthier on paper. The result of the new paper wealth was Americans spent more of their current income and borrowed more. This consumer spending led to stronger economic growth, low inflation, rising profits and later the development of higher stock prices. These higher stock prices attracted trillions of dollars of overseas investment into the United States that stimulated the development of the derivative market.

Because Congress increased demands on financial institutions to loan more money to the "under-served or poor population" the qualification to meet mortgage requirements for home loans were lowered. The result as discussed was the abdication of the traditional lending standards that had existed for a century and the creation of the so-called subprime mortgage market. As mentioned, before 1975 homebuyers who fell into today's subprime category would have been considered too great of a risk by the banks and denied credit because banks were portfolio lenders; they held onto their loans. **To eliminate or minimize their risk created by the subprime loans as a result of Congressional Legislation, lending institutions created the securitization process which involved pooling and repackaging the loans into MBSs and selling them to investors. However, once lending institutions found out how profitable and risk free the subprime market could be as a result of the securitization**

process (MBS), they became addicted to subprime loans and the new lending practices that came with them. This process developed its own culture and became a virus of financial irresponsibility that spread throughout the U.S. and world economies. The purpose of the securitization process (MBS) was designed to allow financial institutions to raise cash from the sale of their current mortgages so they would have the financing to create new mortgages. This process was cyclical allowing the financial institutions to increase their operational cash flow while avoiding financial responsibility and possible losses by selling off their products as MBSs.

With the increase in the number of qualified buyers (with subprime borrowers) for homes and by the lowering of interest rates to all-time lows more people could now afford to buy their dream home. Thus, the combination of six factors led to the contamination of the housing market which became the biggest bubble in history. The six factors were: (1) a change in lending practices by banks, mortgages companies and HUD that were required by Congressional Legislation between 1975-2007, (2) the greed of financial institutions and main street, (3) new economic tools that allowed banks and mortgage companies to spread the risk through bundling loans (MBS) and then transfer the risk to others in the form of Collateralized Debt Obligations CDOs—that are discussed below, (4) historically low interest rates which expanded the housing market, (5) a government philosophy that felt less regulation in the market place was better government, and (6) trillions of dollars of overseas money looking for investments in the United States which created a market for new securities. These six factors provided a major part of the foundation for the perfect financial storm to develop.

As mentioned, an example of one of the **new economic tools** that allowed banks and mortgage companies to spread the risk through securitization (MBS) was called a derivative. One type of derivative that gained popularity in the 1990's was asset-backed commercial paper. This commercial paper led to the development of a new type of derivative called a **credit derivative or (CD).** The value of the credit derivative is **derived** from the **credit risk** on an underlying bond, loan or other financial asset and is designed to transfer **credit risk** from one party to another. One way in which the **credit risk is transferred** and one type of credit derivative is the **Collateralized Debt Obligation** (CDO). CDOs were an important factor in the 2008 financial crisis. A collateralized debt obligation is named for the pooled assets—such as mortgages, bonds and loans—these financial instruments are essentially a debt obligation that serve as collateral for the CDO. The cash flow generated from these assets was repackaged into tranches that were then sold to investors as CDOs. Tranches are pieces of these pooled financial instruments (the income from the mortgages, bonds or loans) that are split up by risk or other characteristics in order to be marketable. Each portion or tranche is one of several related securities offered at the same time but with varying risks, with rewards and maturities to appeal to a diverse range of investors. As an **economic tool** CDOs allowed business speculators to hold and keep assets like mortgages-backed securities (MBS) as collateral and then sell the income stream in the CDO **(transferring the payment risk while the lending institution still owns the mortgage against the assist or home)** from the MBS by creating and selling bonds based on the cash flow from the mortgage interest payments. Investors would then buy a portion of the bond's income (thereby accepting part of the risk) from the mortgage payments according to the investors' **appetite for risk** from the different **credit quality** tiers provided by the credit rating agencies (AAA, AA, down to D—a higher rating was less risk and paid less than a lower rating). The main market participants for CDOs are banks, hedge funds, insurance companies, pension funds and municipalities. Then disaster came as the housing bubble popped and the income from MBSs that were sold as CDO's fell thus causing the credit derivatives (CDOs) to fall in value when monthly mortgage payments were not made. The securitization of the MBSs into credit derivatives (bonds) and the chopping and dicing of these credit derivatives into CDOs was theoretically intended to limit risk and ward off financial problems; but instead, the process which came out of the cultural of financial irresponsibility actually spread risk and magnified the problems of subprime mortgages.

When the Financial Crisis started in 2007 the MBS and CDO process created doubts about the value of the securities and the companies holding them. To make the problem even more complicated another new **economic tool** emerged from the culture of financial irresponsibility called a credit-default swap (CDS). The CDSs were developed to allow the investor to move away from the **risk of investing in interest-rates** (CDO) to the **risk that a borrower would not repay** the mortgage on his home. Thus, credit default swaps (CDSs) are in essence a form of an insurance policy whose value swings with the fiscal health of the asset (CDO) it is written to cover. Because many people felt that housing prices would continue to go up and that people would continue to pay the mortgages on the home they were living in, CDSs were considered a safe investment and were very affordable to purchase. Once the value of the CDOs dropped as mortgages were not paid, companies like AIG (one of the largest insurance companies in the world), that created CDSs to insure (CDOs) incurred huge liabilities. The questions for the financial markets became: (1) how many mortgages defaulted, (2) how many will in the near future in any given CDO, (3) what is the current value of the CDO and (4) could AIG or any other holder of CDSs insurance policies continue to pay for the losses from the CDOs.? Because most of these questions were difficult to answer, the world's credit markets froze. The result was the euphoria surrounding the creation of CDOs and CDSs disappeared and the panic and disaster of which Galbraith wrote ensued and the cycle was complete.

The complications embedded in the MBSs, CDOs, and CDSs, the losses of liquidity and faith in the financial institutions is what Bush 43 had to deal with when he came into office. The problem as he explained in the October 2008 meeting in South Carolina is where do you start and how do you get the liquidity back into the marketplace? This is why he decided that the only way to preserve the free market in the long run was to intervene in the short run---TARP.

History shows that just when society thinks it has developed the **monetary** and **fiscal policies** needed to control the **economic tools** developed by business for speculation such as trust companies, holding-companies, hedge funds and the like; the economic tools fail. Later, new economic tools such as CDOs or CDSs are developed by business for speculation and the process starts all over again. This process is recurring because the business geniuses who developed the new economic tools along mathematical formulas to analyze the impact of their new economic tools think they have solved the market. They believe they developed the Midas touch because technology and circumstances have changed. Thus "it's different this time." But people get greedy, check their brains at the door, and hear what they want to hear as the interaction of human psychology with a market economy practically ensures that history will be ignored and the cycle of euphoria and disaster will continue.

In each cycle of euphoria when new economic tools for speculation are developed society is completely unprepared to deal with the financial impact. The question can be asked: Why is society unprepared? The answer, as demonstrated in our history, society has no way of anticipating the impact of the new economic tools like MBS, CDOs and CDSs on society. Just like society was unprepared to deal with John D. Rockefeller's South Improvement Company and his Standard Oil Trust (the first of its kind) that allowed him and his associates to control 90-95% of the refined oil in the United States by 1879. Nor could the global economy anticipate the impact of a mortgage bond like Jupiter High-Grade CDO V which was owned by Credit Suisse and rated AAA in March of 2007. After receiving a AAA rating on Jupiter, Credit Suisse then sold $1.5 billion in bonds in Jupiter to investors. With that $1.5 billion from Jupiter, Credit Suisse, developed what became a complex pyramid scheme. Jupiter's $1.5 billion was used to buy up pieces of 223 other bonds (which were backed by payments from MBSs) which were made up of the riskiest portions of other bonds (also backed by income from MBSs) which contained subprime mortgages. To make things even more complicated the 223 bonds also owned other bonds. Mantoloking, which was one of the 223 bonds bought by Jupiter, owned parts of 126 other bonds (again backed by income from MBS). But because the subprime mortgages were made against people's homes and Jupiter's investments were spread over 223 bonds with 93% of the bonds being rated AAA by the credit rating agencies; everyone felt their investments were safe and sound. When the subprime market collapsed the questions became who owned what and what were the various 223 bonds worth? What was Jupiter worth? In March 2009, estimates of Jupiter's worth ranged from 5-41 cents on the dollar. # 4 The result was history was replayed with another "**miracle of the creation of money**" which led to another cycle of euphoria and disaster by the creation of new economic tools. A more recent example of the **"miracle of the creation of money"** is Crypto currency.

In October of 2008 the problem facing the Bush administration was the problem facing the banks: determining the value of bonds, like Credit Suisse's Jupiter, and their related assets: MBSsm CDOs, and CDSs. President Bush realized that to be successful TARP had to be timely and flexible in unwinding the financial quagmire created by the Crisis while at the same time accommodating the country's economic needs.

Section: 3

Globalization and its Impact on Global and Domestic Economies

Insight into the problems the globalized financial markets would face in 2007-08 were previewed with the 1997 Asian and the 1998 Russian financial crisis. The Asian financial crisis gripped much of East Asia beginning in July 1997. The crisis raised fears of a worldwide economic meltdown due to financial contagion. Many economists believe that the Asian crisis was not created by market psychology or technology, but by policies that distorted incentives within the lender-borrower relationship. The lender-borrower relationship involved a large quantity of credit that was made available by financial intuitions that became highly leveraged and was used to push up profits and thus asset prices to an unsustainable level. These asset prices eventually became over leveraged, causing individuals and companies to default on their debt obligations.

This globalized impact and potential threat to the U.S. economy prompted the Federal Reserve between 1998-99 to encourage 16 major commercial and investment banks (a combination of U.S. and foreign banks) to pay $3.65 billion to finance a takeover of a major U.S. hedge fund management firm called Long-Term Capital Management LP (LTCM). The Federal Reserve's efforts were not a public bailout—but it did lower interest rates for the 14 of the 16 financial instructions that participated in the takeover. The perfect financial storm was beginning to brew thus exposing the fault lines in the financial system worldwide.

The story of LTCM demonstrates the use of new economic tools that would be used by business for speculation that would lead to economic failures and was a warning of things to come. LTCM was founded in 1994 by John W. Meriwether, the former vice-chairman and head of bond trading at Salomon Brothers. Members of LTCM's board of directors included Myron Scholes and Robert Merton, who shared the 1997 Nobel Memorial Prize in Economics for a "new method to determine the value of derivatives".

Meriwether and his team were **relative-value traders**—a new economic tool. This meant they tracked price relationships between comparable financial instruments looking for price divergences that their mathematical models said were unjustified. An example is the trading spread between new (on-the-run) and old (off-the-run) Treasury bonds. The new or more recently issued bonds usually trade at a slightly higher price to older bonds. The price difference between the new and old bonds would disappear within a short time. The trick is the trader shorts the new bond **(short selling is the sale of a security that is not owned—the shares are borrowed--by the seller and is motivated by the belief that a security's price will decline, enabling it to be bought back at a lower price to make a profit)** and buys the old bonds with the proceeds. By the time the trader closes out the transaction, prices between the old and new bonds normally will have moved back together, and a small profit is made. The price of the bond is not a factor as long as the relative prices of the two bonds move closer together. Making serious money from the small margins in **relative-value trading** requires big positions and heavy leverage. LTCM's leverage ratios were typically in the range of 18-20 to 1. This means with LTMC's $7 billion equity leveraged 18 times they controlled $126 billion in assets. Because investment deals are turned quickly, holding periods are typically short, the interest tab is small. However, if there is a financial crisis and traders cannot turn the deal quickly their losses mount quickly. As the saying goes, relative-value funds "eat like chickens and shit like elephants."

With the help of Merrill Lynch, LTCM secured hundreds of millions of dollars from business owners, celebrities and even private university endowments and later the Italian central bank. The bulk of the money, however, came from companies and individuals connected to the financial industry. LTCM raised $1.25 billion in its investor offering and opened for business in 1994. LTCM's initial success in its first year was over 21% (after fees). During the second and third years the returns respectfully were 43% and 41%. In 1997 profits slipped to 17% and in 1998 LTCM lost $4.6 billion for one four-month period following the 1997 Asian financial crisis and the 1998 Russian financial crisis. The result was investors pulled their money and LTCM had a flight-of-liquidity. In the first three weeks of September 1998, LTCM's equity tumbled from $2.3 billion at the start of the month to just over $400 million by September 25th. With liabilities still over $100 billion, this translated to an effective leverage ratio of more than 250-1, hence the need for assistance from the Federal Reserve.

The effects of globalization and why LTCM finally failed can be illustrated by the Russian financial crisis in 1998. The Russian financial crisis was a product of a number of factors: **(1)** the globalized effect of the Asian financial crisis **(2)** the decline in demand for crude oil and other nonferrous metals (thus price of crude oil and the drop in price of metals caused the cash flow into the Russian economy to decline) that severely impacted the Russian's exchange reserves, **(3)** the Russian government ran up a huge fiscal deficit as a result of the cash shortage which forced them to create a high fixed exchange rate between the ruble and foreign currencies in order to avoid public turmoil. The public turmoil centered on the issues of public wages. In May 1998, coal miners went on strike over unpaid wages and by August 1, 1998, there was approximately $12.5 billion in debt owed to Russian workers, **(4)** inflation reached 84% in Russia, and **(5)** as a result of the Russia's interest payments on its debt, the debt payments rose to a figure 40 percent higher than its monthly tax collections. This situation forced the Russian Central Bank to spend its foreign reserves to defend Russia's currency, which in turn eroded investors' confidence and undermined the ruble even more. In trying to stabilize the situation it is estimated the Russian central bank spent about $27 billion of its U.S. reserves from October 1, 1997, to August 17, 1998, to maintain the floating peg on the ruble. #1

As events leading up to this Russian Crisis developed Western investors panicked, the return rate on Russian Euro-bonds shot up to 90%. This looked like a great opportunity for LTMC who plunged into the market as deeply as possible; thus, further compromising their financial well-being.

The final collapse of LTCM was a result of the combination of economic factors in the Russian economy on August 17, 1998: **(1)** the Russian government defaulted on its GKO Treasury bonds, **(2)** the Russian government also imposed a 90-day moratorium on their foreign debt payments and at the same time abandoned the ruble exchange rate corridor, and **(3)** the Russian Central bank announced that it would stop selling U.S. dollars as the ruble lost 70% of its value against the U.S. dollar. These events signaled the onset to the Russian financial crisis and globalization took its first victim-- LTCM.

Part of the problem for LTCM and the rest of the financial markets is that LTCM's market strategy and new economic tool of **relative-value trading** was copied by other financial institutions. Because LTCM was not the only fund pursuing this strategy as an economic tool, banks were also carrying out similar trades which made the market overbought and when these banks were forced to liquidate their financial instrument it caused the prices to fall dramatically.

When Russian banks defaulted on LTCM and other western financial institutions, the problem for LTCM was they continued to owe a debt to their own clients whose money they leveraged. As these transactions formed a daisy chain with many intermediaries or other financial institutions, and each intermediary had a debt obligation to his/her counterparty (financial institutions they borrowed money from), no simple way could be found to offset the debt obligations of one bank against another. As a result, corporate risk managers throughout Wall Street were forcing all the LTCM and speculative hedge fund look-alikes to dump their positions, regardless of losses. LTCM alone could not sell; its positions were so large they would swamp the marketplace. So, they held on waiting for the price on its positions to turn. When LTCM was forced to fend off margin calls because of the loss of value in their capital base and the magnitude of its existing portfolio, it was forced to liquidate several of its positions at even higher losses. No one had imagined that LTCM had leveraged positions more than $100 billion that was supported by an equity base that had shrunk to only $1 billion by August of 1998. This systemic failure by LTCM and other hedge funds led most market participants to reduce their exposure to emerging markets all around the world, and this caused bank stocks to plummet and the global credit market to enter a panic phase. This globalized financial panic caused individual countries to develop a nationalistic approach by attempting to prevent the exodus of capital from their economies by raising interest rates and placing limits on foreign withdrawal of capital. These policies hurt neighboring countries and added to their financial panic as they were trying to keep their capital markets open.

Many nations learned from the Asian and Russian global financial crisis and quickly built-up foreign exchange reserves as a hedge against any future crisis. However, interestingly enough some nations, such as Brazil, Russia, and India as well as most of East Asia began copying the Japanese model of weakening their currencies and restructuring their economies so as to create a current account surplus to build large foreign currency reserves. This global reaction to the Asian and Russian crisis led to a global influx of cash into the U.S. which helped fuel funding for U.S. treasury bonds. The influx of cash caused the Federal Reserve to lose control over interest rates and aided the stock market bubble of 1996-2000 and the housing market bubble of 2001-2007.

As just mentioned, globalization also influenced domestic economies. Before globalization and the Financial Crisis of 2007-2008 central bankers used the economic tools of short-term interest rates (usually the overnight or federal funds rate) to provide domestic economic stability. These short-term rates did not directly affect the 12-month corporate or 15–30-year mortgage rates. But the links between the short-term and long-term rates were stable enough to allow the central banks to influence the overall financial conditions (by influencing short-term economic behavior by the public) and hence the entire economy. This policy strategy was best summarized by David Blanchflower, a member of the Bank of England's monetary policy committee, as "one tool, one target. The tool was the short-term interest rate, the target was price stability." #2 After globalization these tools were less effective as the Asian and Russian Financial Crisis demonstrated.

In his book "The Age of Turbulence," Alan Greenspan explains the influence of globalization on world economic growth, on inflation and interest rates. From 1989 to 2005, he writes, the number of workers worldwide who engaged in export-oriented industries rose from 300 million to 800 million—a reflection of the entry of China and India into the global economy. All these new workers put down-ward pressure on "wages, inflation, inflation expectation, interest rates, and accordingly significantly contributed to rising world economic growth." # 3

As a result of these down-ward pressures from globalization the links between short-term and long-term rates became fractured. A disconnect developed between short-term and long-term rates as a result of the record level of saving worldwide and the global financial trends. These global financial trends such as record levels of savings, low inflation, and world economic stability allowed foreign investors to pour their savings into U.S. stocks, bonds and other new financial assets. **The global influx of cash helped keep interest rates low and prompted lenders to extend more credit to homeowners. This led to an even more global influx of cash which caused long-term interest and mortgage rates to fall even further and caused the Federal Reserve, at this point, to lose control over mortgage rates. As rates declined, people shifted funds into the stock market and later into housing.** Share prices and home values rose, making Americans wealthier. Many Americans substituted this added paper wealth in their homes for annual savings. They spent more from their current income and borrowed more. When mortgage rates continued to fall this prompted homeowners to refinance repeatedly using their homes as ATMs. In 1982, the personal savings rate was 11 percent of disposable income; by 2005, the "culture of consumption" brought the saving rate down to near zero. Changes in legislation and in the financial industry (discussed earlier) allowed banks to make loans to low-income households which made homeownership in the U.S.

rise to **69**% by 2004. #4 Lenders no longer held and maintained the loans they made because they could now sell them off into a secondary market and limit their liability. The foundation for this financial practice (as we discussed) was created in part by various acts of Congress. As mentioned, the AMTPA of 1982 helped create the "culture of financial irresponsibility" and the tools for predatory lending by allowing the development of a variety of short-term mortgages with adjustable-rates, balloon payments, and negative amortization that enabled home buyers to pay higher prices while temporarily making low monthly payments. As the housing market kept booming, it allowed the great American shopping spree and the economy to continue the boom.

As the Federal Reserve had primed the economic pump, factors tied to globalization that were beyond their control would not allow them to turn it off. The Federal Reserve lost control of interest rates and thus the economy as a result of Globalization of the money market and the development of new mathematical models looking for price divergences with the use of "short selling" and the creation of new economic tools like **relative-value trading.**

Section: 4

Alan Greenspan and the Federal Reserve Board Policies

As mentioned before and a key concept of Galbraith's economic policy: "To see economic policy as a problem of choice between rival ideologies is the greatest error of our time." # 1 (Galbraith Money p. 305) This quote can be exemplified by evaluating the actions of Federal Reserve Chairman Alan Greenspan who served as Chairman from 1987-2006. Before Greenspan retired, he was proclaimed "the greatest central banker who ever lived". He was awarded the Presidential Medal of Freedom, the French Legion of Honor, and was knighted by the British. Greenspan explains the reason behind his ideology and theory of self-regulating markets with the following quote:

"As a bank regulator for more than eighteen years, I came to recognize that government regulation cannot substitute for individual integrity. In fact, any form of government guarantees of credit lessens the need of financial counterparties to earn a reputation for honest dealings. It is conceivable, of course, that government guarantees are superior to an individual's reputation. But guarantees—even the most widely praised, such as deposit insurance—have costly consequences. I concluded, and I suspect most regulators agree, that the first and most effective line of defense against fraud and insolvency is counterparties, surveillance. For example, JP Morgan thoroughly scrutinizes the balance sheet of Merrill Lynch before it lends. It does not look to the Securities and Exchange Commission to verify Merrill's solvency." # 2

As an economist Greenspan believed as Adam Smith had advocated that if man followed his own self-interests, he would realize that his greatest good would be gained not through the exploitation of his fellow man, but through a recognition of his duties and obligations to society. In Greenspan's case it was banking officials protecting their shareholders from bad loan decisions. But in Greenspan's October 23, 2008, testimony before the "(Commission)" he said he made a "mistake in believing that banks, operating in their own self-interest, would do what was necessary to protect their shareholders and institutions". He called the financial crisis a "once-in-a century credit tsunami" that led to the breakdown in the free market system. # 3

However, Greenspan seemed to forget that the period from the late 1980's to 2002 saw four other boom-and-bust cycles. The first was the big crash in residential mortgages in 1994. The second and third were two big trading-based crises –the 1987 stock market crash and the 1998 Long-Term Capital Management crisis (LTCM). As mentioned at one point during the LTCM crisis the Federal Reserve thought the crisis might bring down the major global financial markets. A week before the LTCM crisis Greenspan told Congress, "Market pricing and counterparty surveillance can be expected to do most of the job of sustaining safety and soundness." Later Greenspan said the financial meltdown had revealed a flaw in his lifetime of economic thinking and left him in a "state of shocked disbelief**".** # 4 He concluded by saying that fear by investors has at least three times the effect of euphoria in producing market gyrations.

The fourth crisis was the dot-com bubble that developed between 1997-2002 and produced a period of excessive speculation in companies that specialized in the usage and adaptation of the Internet by businesses and consumers. During the 1997-2002 period valuations of companies in the dot-com industry increased rapidly. The dot-com peak was reached in March of 2000 and the bubble had collapsed by 2002. The reason behind the collapse was the virus of "financial irresponsibility". Venture capitalists, eager to profit from this new frontier in technology, moved in irresponsible ways to raise capital faster and with less caution than usual. A combination of four factors helped create the environment and mindset for "financial irresponsibility." The factors which helped create the mindset were: (1) rapidly increasing stock prices, (2) market confidence that the companies would turn future profits, (3) widely available venture capital provided by the Federal Reserve and Greenspan between 1998-1999 with their low-interest rate environment, and (4) speculation in stocks by individuals which came about as a result of the first three factors.

In January of 2001 when Greenspan saw that the economy was sputtering under the dotcom boom he convened a conference call of the central bank's top policymakers. They agreed to cut the Fed's benchmark short-term interest rate for the first time in two years, to 6 percent from 6.5 percent. This action started an aggressive campaign by Greenspan and the Fed to prevent an economic downturn.

Greenspan had studied the Great Depression of the 1930's and believed it resulted largely from the Fed's mistakes in tightening credit after the 1929 stock market crash. Greenspan had also seen Japan's central bank ease credit too cautiously after that country's property bubble burst in the early 1990's, triggering a decade-long economic slump. He wanted to do the opposite, dramatically easing credit—to cushion the economic landing.

Greenspan and the Fed lowered its benchmark rate another 12 times from January 2001 to June 2003. By June 2003 the rate was one percent, the lowest level since 1959. The benchmark rate is the overnight rate on loans between banks and it influences many other longer-term rates in the economy. The rate includes those on mortgages, car loans and business loans. Low interest rates encourage consumers and businesses to borrow and spend which stimulates economic growth.

Greenspan's plan worked as household spending rose in 2001, 2002, and 2004. The recession was one of the mildest on record as the economy started growing in November 2001 and continued until the Financial Crisis in 2007. As a result of the recovery, Greenspan suggested that more homeowners should consider taking out adjustable-rate mortgages (ARMs) where the interest rate adjusts itself to the current interest rate in the market. This was a **HUGE MISTAKE** on Greenspan's part. At the time of Greenspan's suggestion, the Fed's benchmark rate was at an all-time-low of 1 percent. A few months after his recommendation, the Fed began raising interest rates, in a series of rate hikes that would bring the benchmark rate to 5.25 percent over the next 2 years. A major factor in the 2007 subprime mortgage crisis was many subprime ARMs would reset at much higher interest rates than what the borrowers could afford to pay or believed they would have to pay.

Besides recommending ARMs or "mortgage product alternatives" over traditional fixed-rate mortgages; Greenspan in an April 8, 2005, speech praised the rise of the subprime mortgage industry and its tools for assessing creditworthiness:

"Innovation has brought about a multitude of new products, such as subprime loans and niche credit programs for immigrants. Such developments are representative of the market responses that have driven the financial services industry throughout the history of our country.... With these advances in technology, lenders have taken advantage of credit-scoring models and other techniques for efficiently extending credit to a broader spectrum of consumers. ... Where once more marginal applicants would simply have been denied credit, lenders are now able to quite efficiently judge the risk posed by individual applicants and to price that risk appropriately. These improvements have led to rapid growth in subprime mortgage lending; indeed, today subprime mortgages account for roughly 10 percent of the number of all mortgages outstanding, up from just 1 or 2 percent in the early 1990s." # 5

Some critics, and rightfully so, blame Greenspan for laying the foundation to the financial crisis by lowering interest rates too low for too long which created huge imbalances in the domestic and global economies. This criticism was expressed even before he retired on January 31, 2006. In 2004 a Businessweek magazine analysts argued against Greenspan: "It was the Federal Reserve-engineered decline in rates that inflated the housing bubble...the most troublesome aspect of the price run-up is that many recent buyers are squeezing into houses that they can barely afford by taking advantage of the lower rates available from adjustable-rate mortgages. That leaves them fully exposed to rising rates." # 6 Another critic Nell Henderson from the Washington Post states in a February 5, 2006, article: "… his legacy will be judged not just by his record at the Fed, but also by the economy he bequeaths. And when he leaves office Jan. 31, Greenspan leaves a nation awash in debt---record household debt and a record trade gap." # 7 Greenspan's defense of his policies and that of his Fed colleagues about the economy they bequeathed is---that part of the growth in household debt and the trade gap were side effects of policies that helped steady the U.S. economy after the stock market bubble burst in 2000. Thus between 2000-2004, the Fed developed a low-interest rate policy that encouraged the "culture of consumption" by encouraging consumers to borrow and spend on houses, autos and other goods, spurring economic growth for several years while businesses were cutting jobs and reluctant to invest. As consumers spent much of their borrowed money on imports, they caused the trade deficit to swell to a record level. The Federal Reserve felt the alternative would have been worse—a longer and more painful downturn or a Japan-like decade of economic stagnation. By mid-2004 the Fed saw possible problems developing in the economy and tried to change course by raising the short-term or benchmark rate and expected that the longer-term rate, such as mortgages, would rise as well, causing consumers to borrow less and save more. However, it didn't work out that way because capital from overseas kept pouring into the country in order to take advantage of the financial opportunities that the MBS and the CDOs had created—thus overseas capital put a downward pressure on interest rates even as Greenspan and the Fed tried to raise them.

The earlier four boom-and-bust cycles were just a warmup for the 2007-2008 Financial Crisis. All four of the cycles arose from a fundamental change in investment strategies which were influenced by the virus of "financial irresponsibility" and carried out by technologies which were enabled by breakthroughs in mathematical formulas. The result was assets could now be carved up and reassembled into new products with little **apparent risk** to fit investor needs. This process led to a very wide range of complex, structured investment instruments like CDOs, CDSs and MBS, just to mention a few, that revolutionized wholesale banking and Wall Street itself. All of the new technologies and strategies, which were backed by the Federal Reserve and Alan Greenspan's theory of self-regulating markets, harbored dangerous flaws that tended to reveal themselves only at points of great stress.

Hindsight is always said to be twenty-twenty. As mentioned, Timothy Geithner said: "In these circumstances, you don't have perfect foresight." # 8 The question becomes: considering Greenspan's successful record, with his same knowledge and opportunity under the same circumstances would Greenspan or anyone else in his position have done anything different? It is true that some people forecast that the debt burden and the housing boom would lead to economic calamity, but many of those Jeremiahs had been predicting disaster for a decade.

Greenspan's theory of a free-market economy would have worked during the 2007-2008 Financial Crisis, the markets could have corrected themselves, but the human cost and pain would have been so great on the general population that the government would have had to step in to soften the pain. As FDR once said during the Great Depression; "Government has a final responsibility for the well-being of its citizens. If a private cooperative endeavor fails to provide work for willing hands and relief for the unfortunate, those suffering hardship from no fault of their own have a right to call upon the Government for aid; and a government worthy of its name must make a fitting response." # 9 The lesson is that although many theories sound logical and will work, they always must be adjusted for an ever-changing environment and the human factor--GREED. Making the correct adjustment to produce a sound economy is a major role of the federal government since the New Deal. As FDR had said: "…a government worthy of its name must make a fitting response" just as TARP and Bush's "all-in policy" was the "fitting response" for the country in 2008.

Section: 5

The Rating Agencies

Credit rating agencies play a key role in structured financial transactions such as asset-backed securities (ABS), mortgage-backed securities (MBS), commercial mortgage-backed securities (CMBS), and collateralized debt obligations (CDOs). The rating agency industry is a highly concentrated industry, with the "Big Three" credit rating agencies controlling approximately 95% of the rating business. Moody's and Standard & Poor's together control 80% of the **global market**, and Fitch Ratings controls another15%. These three agencies are not the only sources of credit information. Many smaller rating agencies also exist, mostly serving non-US markets. #1

Credit reporting and the credit rating system in the United States developed as a result of a four-phase process. The **first phase** involved credit reporting and developed after the Panic of 1837 to evaluate the ability of a business to pay their bills. The **second phase** expanded on the first phase by collecting information on what kind of assets a business owned (in this case the railroads who created a complex national transportation system) and how strong the business was financially. No opinion was given at this time it was up to the purchaser of the information to evaluate it for themselves. The **third phase** developed when a professional opinion was given as to the quality of the assists being evaluated, which led to the final **phase** when the quality of the assets was given a professional rating from AAA to D.

As mentioned, business or mercantile credit reporting agencies were established in the wake of the financial crisis of 1837. During this first phase agencies reported on the ability of **individual merchants** to pay their debts and consolidated the merchant's business information for investors in their published guides. The first such agency was established in 1841 by Lewis Tappan in New York City. Tappan's agency was acquired by Robert G. Dun who immediately changed the name of the company to RG Dun & Co. and published his first credit guide to assess the creditworthiness of individual merchants in 1859. John M. Bradstreet had formed his agency in 1849 providing the same services as Dun. In 1933, the John M Bradstreet Company merged with Dun Company to form today's Dun & Bradstreet.

Credit ratings of financial instruments trace their roots back to the late 1840s with the development of large financial markets as a result of the building of western railroads and the canal systems. Before western expansion and the development of national markets, business owners were close to those who purchased goods or services from them. It was easy for the merchants to extend credit to them due to their proximity and the fact that the merchants knew their customers personally and knew whether or not they would be able to pay them back. As trading distances increased and the development of the railroads led to the creation of a national market, merchants no longer personally knew their customers and became leery of extending credit to people who they did not know in fear of not being paid back. The traditional means of obtaining information via family business and banking relationships became insufficient. Investors wanted independent, third-party information upon which to make investment and pricing decisions. Business owners' hesitation to extend credit to new customers led to the development of the **first phase** and birth of the credit reporting industry.

The development of an extensive railroad system led to the development of corporate bonds being issued to finance them, and therefore a bond market developed in the United States that was several times larger than in any other country. This led to the development of the **second phase** of the credit rating industry. In response to the financial market's need to finance railroad construction Henry Varnum Poor, who became editor of the American Railroad Journal in 1849, started to publish systematic information on the property of railroads, their assets, liabilities and earnings. It was up to the individual or company purchasing the report to evaluate the information provided. The Journal proved to be so popular with investors that after the Civil War in 1865, Poor and his son started their own publication on railroads. Poor's Manual on the railroads became the industry's authoritative source for several decades and was the forerunner of modern-day credit ratings.

In 1909 John Moody took the publication of credit information a step further when he developed **phase three.** Moody created the first credit rating agency to publish an **opinion on the creditworthiness** of the corporate debt (bonds) of the railroads. Moody's opinions were based on extensive company and industry information and rigorous analysis.

The Poor Company followed Moody's lead in 1916 and added an opinion on the creditworthiness to their reports. In 1941, Poor Publishing merged with Standard Statistics Bureau, another information and rating company to form Standard & Poor's. The idea was to provide financial information on non-railroad companies.

Fitch Publishing Company started publishing financial information in 1913 and in 1924 introduced the final phase of the current rating system of "AAA" to "D" ratings on the quality of assets held by a company.

The stock market crash of 1929 sparked a greater demand for credit ratings as investors worried about high bond defaults rates and credit risk, thus from this point on the majority of bonds issued were rated by the rating agencies. **In 1931 the U.S. Treasury Department adopted credit ratings as a measure of the quality of the bonds held by national banks. This practice was quickly adopted by other business and financial institutions and, soon relying on credit ratings became the norm.**

In the 1970s rating agencies began to expand ratings of securities to firms other than a few large established blue-chip corporations. Rating agencies also began to apply their ratings beyond bonds to counterparty risks, the performance risk of mortgage servicers, and the price volatility of mutual funds and mortgage-back securities. The complexity of the **new economic tools** that were financially engineered by the use of mathematical formulas such as subprime mortgage-backed securities (MBS), collateralized debt obligations (CDO) and synthetic CDOs—were difficult to understand and to price. For example, to determine the risk or likely returns, investors had to calculate the statistical probabilities that certain kinds of mortgages might default, and to estimate the revenues that would be lost because of those defaults. Then investors would have to determine the effect of the losses on the payments to different **tranches** in the bond. A good example of the complexity of this process was discussed earlier with the Jupiter High-Grade CDO V mortgage bond. As discussed, Jupiter was a $1.5 billion dollar bond that was used to buy up pieces of 223 other bonds (which were backed by payments from MBSs) which were made up of the riskiest portions of other bonds (also backed by income from MBSs) which contained subprime mortgages. **Because of the complexity of this process and the amount of financial knowledge needed to understand this process everyone outsourced their risk management to the rating agencies**. It is at this point that Greenspan's axiom of government regulation versus individual integrity runs into problems. The complexity of the MBs, CDOs, CDSs forced investors to rely solely on the rating agencies and their individual integrity as companies. But the rating agencies didn't follow John Moody's example of giving an opinion or rating based on extensive company and industry information and rigorous analysis. There were no other "counterparties to provide surveillance" as Greenspan had advocated and the ratings assigned by the big 3 were accepted as fact. The result was the rating of these new structured financial instruments became a great source of revenue for the agencies. Competition was tough between the Big Three and profits were great, so the practice which was eventually developed by the agencies was to give the companies what they wanted— triple A ratings. By 2006 Moody's had earned $881 million in revenue from rating the new economic tools. Between 2004—2009 the profit margin for the Big Three was up about 50%. # 2

Rating agencies were in the business of evaluating investment bonds and deciding if they would be repaid on time and in full. Rating agencies are needed because bonds are not traded on public exchanges, and most of the information about them is held by investment bankers and traders who are trying to sell them. Once the quality of a bond is determined the agencies use a series of letter grades to rate the bonds. A triple-A rating means that the bond has the same risk of default as a U.S. Treasury bond—almost nil. Next, are the double-A to triple-B ratings that are still considered investment grade and safe enough for pension funds and other institutional investors. Finally, there are the "junk" bonds which are illegal for pension funds and other institutional investors to own. Thus, the business of rating agencies was not only to evaluate the quality of investments for potential investors but to create an evaluation that could be trusted by all in the marketplace; consequently, everyone assumed that a triple-A rating was triple-A.

The housing bubble in all likelihood would not have occurred if the private rating agencies like Moody's, Standard & Poor's and Fitch, had not rubber-stamped mortgage-backed securities and CDOs which contained subprime loans with triple-A ratings. The significance of these agencies was that investors as well as lenders trusted and relied on these agencies to decide what securities to purchase for their retirement programs or in the case of lenders to evaluate the collateral, they would make loans against. The difficulty for the rating agencies as mentioned was how do you calculate the statistical probability that a certain kind of mortgage might default and what that lost income would be. Also how do you then determine the loss of payments to the different tranches with any given bond that was made up from different qualities of mortgages from prime to subprime. The solution for the "Big Three" rating agencies was to sidestep the process and rate many of the bond's triple-A.

When the Financial Crisis hit and losses started surfacing in even highly rated mortgage-related securities, lenders and investors realized they could no longer trust or rely on the ratings assigned by the rating agencies to any mortgage-related securities. Because lenders were unable to evaluate the risks of complex securities on their own, they pulled back from lending against any type of security that included any amount of subprime risk. In 2007 because of: (1) the globalizations of the financial markets and (2) **as a result of the lack of trust in the rating of securities by the agencies a wave of panicky selling developed in markets around the world thus deepening the Financial Crisis.** Investors were realizing that they did not know: (1) exactly who held subprime-related securities, (2) had little reliable information about the loans that backed those securities, and (3) could not anticipate which financial entity might be next to deny them access to their money.

The purpose of mortgage-back securities and CDOs was to take assets that could never merit a triple-A rating on their own and modify them into assets that could be triple-A rated. Like everyone else on Wall Street, rating agencies used mathematical formulas and the idea of diversification to spread the risk to create probability models in determining the rating of their bonds. In 2001 Standard & Poor's developed the practice of packaging up to 20 percent of second home mortgages into a pool of residential mortgage-backed securities (RMBS) and rating the bond as having no additional risk. The justification for rating agencies and lending institutions had for this practice was that the risk was low because housing prices were continuing to go up and the mathematical formulas showed the risk default of the second and subprime mortgages would be spread over a large geographical area. The same justification was used to make subprime "piggyback mortgages" (A loan in which the homeowner takes out two loans—one for the first mortgage and the other would cover the down payment.). These mortgages would be sold and were bundled into bonds that were rated investment grade. One bond might contain as many as ten thousand mortgages. If all of the mortgages came from California the risk was higher, but if part of the mortgages came from California, some from Texas, and others from Connecticut and Hawaii then the risk was so diversified the bond was believed to be safe because it was unlikely that a recession would hit all of those states at the same time. Thus, subprime mortgage-back securities that were bundled into a triple-B rating could now be sliced and diced into tranches with some triple-A mortgages and packaged into CDOs and receive a Triple-A rating, as discussed with Jupiter High- Grade CDO V mortgage bonds. # 3

On April 23, 2010, a former Managing Director at Standard and Poor's (Frank Raiter) testified before the Senate Subcommittee investigating the Financial Crisis: "...completive pressures between rating agencies and pressure on analysts by management to earn fees from financial institutions led agencies to award high rating to risky investments." Raiter stated the analysts were told to perform or quit. A Senior vice President in the derivative products group at Moody's who was employed by them from 1999 until he resigned in 2010 stated: "... that analysts whose conclusions prevented Moody's clients from getting what they needed were viewed as "impeding deals" and thus harming Moody's business. These analysts were often transferred, disciplined or fired." # 4 Moody's greatly profited from rating mortgage-back securities. Revenue soared from $600 million in 2000 to $2.2 billion in 2007. # 5 During the debacle of the Financial Crisis 73% or over $800 billion worth of mortgage-backed securities that Moody's had rated triple-A in 2006 were downgraded to junk status by 2008.

Another problem with this whole process is that in many cases **the rating agencies were not verifying the information contained in the residential mortgage-backed securities (MBS) and there was no legal requirement for them to do so.** Once a mortgage-backed security was stamped triple-A, nobody ever went back and verified the financial information when RMBS were re-bundled into a CDOs. Because of the complexity of the MBS, CDOs, and bonds **everyone simply assumed that a triple-A rating was triple-A.** An example of this dependency can be demonstrated by using the actions of the school board in Whitefish Bay, Wisconsin. The school board felt their teachers' retirement plan was underfunded so they turned to a local investment banker who had been advising them for two decades.

Investment Banker, David Noack, from Stifel, Nicolaus & Company, a St. Louis investment Bank had little knowledge of how the complicated CDO's worked, but Noack made representations to the Whitefish Bay school board that he did. Noack knew that the CDOs were triple-A rated and that was all he needed to know. Noack informed the school board that the CDO's were triple-A rated and that was all they needed to know---they were as safe as US Treasuries. Consequently, the school board members never read the 3" thick prospectus because: "We had all our questions answered satisfactorily by Dave Noack, so I wasn't worried." # 6 To the defense of the school board members they did not have the background or knowledge about financial investments of this type to make an evaluation. Their judgment was based on what David Noack told them, after all Noack had been advising them for 20 years. Stifel, Nicolaus & Company received $1.2 million for putting the deal together and David Noack salary as a broker was about $300,000 per year.

The CDOs were constructed by the Royal Bank of Canada. The bank had a relationship with Stifel, Nicolaus & Company which sold $200 million worth of collateralized debt obligation (CDO's.) to the Whitefish Bay Board and 4 other districts. The Royal Bank of Canada received promises of payments from the Whitefish Bay school board totaling about $11.2 million.

The 5 districts together borrowed $165 million from **Depfa Bank** (Depfa Bank provides banking, financial, and related services to public sector clients worldwide) and the districts contributed $35 million of its own money. The CDO's were described by Mr. Noack as a collection of bonds from 105 of the most reputable companies that would pay the school board a small return every quarter. The problem was that Mr. Noack didn't know what he was selling. The school's $200 ($165 plus $35) million was used as collateral for an insurance guarantee on about $20 billion of corporate bonds for CDOs. The CDOs would pay the school district about 1 percent more in interest on $165 million they borrowed; plus, they would receive interest on their own $35 million. In essence, the school districts were acting like a bank: borrowing money at one rate and lending it out at a higher one. If none of the bonds defaulted, the schools would receive about $1.8 million a year after paying off their own debt. By comparison, the $200 million on the corporate CDO bonds offered only a modestly better return than the $35 million investment in ultra-safe Treasury bonds, which would have paid about $1.5 million a year, with virtually no risk." "If just six percent of the bonds insured went bad, the Wisconsin educators could lose all their money." # 7

The good news for the five school districts and the Whitefish Bay school board was their three-and-a-half-year lawsuit led to them recovering all their money. The final settlement in the case was $217.9 million, which included $63.9 million in cash and $154 million in debt forgiveness.

The problem for society, as well as the Wisconsin school districts, was the development of new structured financial products like MBS and CDOs that led to the creation of a new culture of **financial irresponsibility.** In the old culture Greenspan's idea of reputation and integrity mattered; the rating agencies worried more about their reputation than they did about market share. For many of the rating agency executives, the expansion of the structured financial products market and the large profits that could be made for rating these products, plus the stock options and bonus that could be received, became more important than the integrity or reputation of their company. The increase in the number of triple-A ratings reflects the impact of the new culture of "financial irresponsibility". In mid-2006 there were only nine private-sector companies in the world which carried a triple-A rating. By January 2008, there were 64,000 structured financial instruments rated triple-A. There were also many other financial investments that had investment-grade ratings. By 2010 there were only 5 triple-A rated companies in the world. # 8 What made the creation of the new culture so easy was the conflict of interest that surrounded the rating agencies. The rating agencies are paid for their services by the seller or issuer of the bond so their loyalty is not to the buyer, but to the small group of investment bankers who created the bonds. Keeping this point in mind, as well as: (1) remembering that investors generally outsourced their due diligence to the rating agencies, (2) investors would not buy a bond unless it was rated, and (3) once a bond was rated, the rating was universally accepted-- it is little wonder this Ponzi scheme by the rating agencies helped create the financial crisis of 2007-2008. **Senator Carl Levin, D-Michigan, who was chairmen of the subcommittee investigating the financial crisis stated: "Had credit rating agencies**

been more careful in issuing ratings or downgraded ratings in a more responsible manner, maybe we would have averted the crisis." Levin continued by saying: "… that once the crisis became apparent the rating agencies failed to acknowledge the problems fast enough; thus, triggering mass downgrades of billions in investments, shocking the financial system which in turn created panic that added to the crisis" # 9

Other critics of the rating agencies point out there was no accountability of the agencies for the different financial disasters they helped create or did not detect until it was too late. These include the 1970 Penn Central bankruptcy, the 1976 New York City fiscal crisis, the 1994 Orange County default, the 1997 Asian and Russian financial crises, the 1998 collapse of the Long-Term capital Management hedge fund, the 2001 Enron and WorldCom bankruptcies and finally the 2007-08 subprime mortgage crisis. The way the system was supposed to work under the rating agencies was: (1) the agencies would provide ongoing reviews of securities after their initial rating and (2) they could and should change a security's rating if they felt its creditworthiness had changed. Rating agencies typically signaled in advance their intention to reconsider rating changes. The "Big Three" all used negative "outlook" notifications to indicate the potential for a downgrade. Negative "outlook" notifications are used to indicate that a downgrade is likely within the next 90 days

In 2001, during the Enron accounting scandal; the company's investment ratings remained the same by the rating agencies until four days before their bankruptcy—even though Enron's stock had been in sharp decline for several months as a result of fraudulent practices having been revealed. Critics complained that not a single analyst at S&P or Moody's lost their jobs as a result of not exposing Enron's fraudulent practices. The rating agencies response to the Enron situation should have been to issue a negative "outlook". The notification would indicate a potential downgrade was likely within the next 90 days. This lack of attention and accountability continued during the subprime crisis, when hundreds of billions of dollars' worth of triple-A rated mortgage-backed securities were abruptly downgraded from triple-A to "junk" status within two years of being issued. Again, the "Big Three" rating agencies were not held accountable. Another example of the agency's ineffectiveness is demonstrated when Moody's continued to rate Freddie Mac's preferred stock triple-A until mid-2008 when it was downgraded to one tick above junk bond status.

When Dodd-Frank became law in July 2010 it stipulated that the rating agencies assigning grades to asset-backed securities be subject to expert liability from the moment the asset was rated. This opened the rating agencies to lawsuits from investors. **However, the S.E.C. rules state rating agencies are not subject to expert liability. The rating agencies have escaped legal liability by claiming their ratings are protected by the First Amendment right to free speech.** # 10 The rating agency problem could be solved by eliminating the conflict-of-interest problem by having the buyers of the financial instruments becoming the clients of the rating agencies instead of the financial instructions that are selling the bonds.

In his book "The Age of Turbulence" Greenspan explains the importance of trust in the Marketplace and by extension the rating agencies.

Reputation and the trust it fosters have always appeared to me to be the core required attributes of market capitalism. Laws at best can prescribe only a small fraction of the day-by-day activities in the marketplace. When trust is lost, a nation's ability to transact business is palpably undermined. In the marketplace, uncertainties created by not always truthful counterparties raise credit risk and thereby increase real interest rates. # 11

Section: 6

The Greed of Main Street and Wall Street

The foundation of the Financial Crisis was built on a laudable attempt at social engineering home ownership for the "under-served or poor populations." The extended consequences of social engineering home ownership were not laudable. The consequences feed the greed of both Main Street and Wall Street.

The Panic and Financial Crisis of 2007-2008 has critics on both sides of the political and economic spectrum pointing fingers at each other. In order to better understand the cause of the Financial Crisis, Congress created a ten-member commission called the America's Financial Crisis Inquiry Commission or "The Commission". The findings of "The Commission" were 3-fold. The first view held by only one member of "The Commission", a Republican, places the blame squarely on government policies aimed at increasing home ownership among the "under-served or poor populations". The second view, an opinion supported by three of the remaining Republicans on "The Commission" states that everyone was to blame. This included politicians, regulators, bankers, and homebuyers alike who grew too relaxed about debt and leverage. This view stresses broad economic dynamics, placing less emphasis on Wall Street and deregulation.

The final opinion supported by all six Democrats on the "Commission" was that the crisis occurred because of the financial industry's greed and sloppy risk management. However, this greed and sloppy risk management was supported by politicians who for a quarter-century passed deregulation legislation that allowed Wall Street to run wild.

What is forgotten by the six Democrats on "The Commission" is that the same greed that engulfed Wall Street was present on Main Street. The only difference was that the people on Wall Street were playing with bigger numbers which by their very nature created a much bigger impact. Some might say it is hard to compare the greed of hedge fund managers who are playing with millions and in some cases billions of dollars to a person who has lied about his or her income or signed documents that mortgage companies put forth that misrepresented their income so they could qualify to buy a house they could not afford. Similarly, there were individuals who bought several houses with little or no money down betting that the price of housing would continue to rise and they would "flip" the houses for a quick profit and start all over again. In both cases it was the same poison- greed – that killed the economy**. The strength of Wall Street's poison came from the large amount of money they were leveraging within the system; while the strength of the poison from Main Street came from the large number of transactions in the form of subprime loans and loans that were based on predatory lending practices that were injected into the system.**

Greenspan finally recognized the error of his ways and the effects of the poison pill when he admitted to the "Commission" in October of 2008 that he had made a "mistake in believing that banks, operating in their own self-interest, would do what was necessary to protect their shareholders and institutions." Following one's own enlightened self-interest means a person can see the "big picture", that is, his self-interest is best served by providing the best product or service that will meet not only his needs but needs of his customers. In the 1970s and early 80s financial institutions' self-interest were tied to the mortgages they created and expected to hold for a long time. But with the new generation of mortgage banks and financial practices that emerged in the 1980s and 90s, financial institutions developed an attitude of "financial irresponsibility" which led to a different view of their self-interest.

The new view of self-interest was processing as many loans as possible regardless of their quality and then selling them off within a few months and not having the responsibility of holding the loans for years to come. As former Secretary of the Treasury Paul O'Neal once stated, if society would have stuck to the old practice of 20% down there might not have been a housing bubble or a Financial Crisis.

In raising the question of the financial industry's greed and sloppy risk management "The Commission," ignored what history has shown, that the passions of men will not conform to reason. Historically, checks upon human nature and its tendency to abuse power as reflected in the greed of Wall Street and Main Street were, in some ways, provided for in our Constitution. The Founding Fathers believed that human nature was universally fallible, and only built-in institutional safeguards could be counted on to counter man's human nature and ambitions. James Madison who is considered the father of our Constitution once stated:

> "… ambition must be made to counteract ambition. The interest of the man must be connected with the constitutional rights of the place. It may be a reflection on human nature that such devices should be necessary to control the abuses of government. But what is government itself but the greatest of all reflections on human nature? If men were angels, no government would be necessary. If angels were to govern men, neither external nor internal controls on government would be necessary." # 1

Although Madison was speaking politically about human nature, the concept also applies to man's human nature and ambitions in following his own economic self-interest. When pushed too far, human nature 's economic self-interest becomes **greed** as seen from our first financial crisis in 1792 and continued up to the 2007-2008 Financial Crisis. It has been said, speculators as a species will never die. However, some have argued that greed is not an accurate phrase to describe the actions of man's human nature found in Main Street or Wall Street. Instead, they would claim the actions of Main Street and Wall Street were based on rational behavior. The argument that human history seems to support is that if incentives are established either intentionally or unintentionally as demonstrated during the Financial Crisis, it is rational for people to act upon those incentives. Thus, the problem becomes; how does society control man's rational behavior (following his own self-interest) so that it supports the public good?

In applying Madison's theory on human nature to the Financial Crisis, in framing a government that will control financial irresponsibility and guide the development of the economy, which is to be administered by men over men, the great difficulty lies in this: you must first enable the government to control man's ambitions and human nature as had developed on Wall Street; and in the next place oblige it to control the same ambitions as found in human nature in Main Street.

The virus of the culture of "financial irresponsibility" developed under the stewardship of the Federal Government which involved both Democrats and Republicans. Everyone drank the Kool-Aid and believed as Galbraith would say they had developed the Midas touch with the development of the new mathematical methods and economic tools. But the "kit of tools" did not solve the problems found in the lessons of history which exposed the flaws of human nature as played out as the cycle of euphoria and panic repeated itself in the Financial Crisis of 2007-2008.

Section: 7

The Role of Fannie Mae

Fannie Mae was established under the New Deal program by an amendment to the National Housing Act of 1934 that was designed to assist in the construction, acquisition, and rehabilitation of residential properties during the Great Depression. The Depression wrought havoc on the US housing market. By 1933, an estimated 20 to 25 % of the nation's outstanding mortgage debt was in default. Fannie Mae's explicit purpose was to provide local banks with federal money to finance home mortgages in an attempt to raise the levels of home ownership and the availability of affordable housing. Fannie Mae created a liquid secondary mortgage market by purchasing mortgages back from approved mortgage sellers, and then securitized them by packaging them into mortgage-back securities (MBS) and then selling them to investors in the secondary mortgage market. This process made it possible for banks and other loan originators to issue more housing loans. Because of the long-term nature of mortgages, the secondary market (where financial institutions can sell their loans after they are made) is an essential factor in maintaining lender liquidity which allows mortgage originators to replenish their funds, which can then be used for additional loans. This practice was expanded on, as discussed, as result of the actions of HUD and the 10 Congressional Legislative Acts which established new requirements that led to subprime loans and relaxed lending requirements. This financial environment encouraged lending institutions to convert all of their loans into MBS's and sell them off into the secondary markets. If the banks had to keep all these mortgages the full 15 or 30 years, they would soon use up most of their funds and make it difficult for home buyers to find a mortgage lender. For the first thirty years following its inception, Fannie Mae held a monopoly over the secondary mortgage market. Originally, Fannie had an 'explicit guarantee' from the government; if Fannie Mae got in trouble, the government promised to bail it out. This changed in 1968.

In 1968 the Federal government laid the foundation for another event that contributed to the development of the **"Perfect Storm"** when it "converted Fannie Mae into a publicly held corporation called a Government-Sponsored Enterprise (GSE). The justification for the Federal government conversion was to remove Fannie Mae's activity--its financial responsibility and debt from the federal budget. What in effect happened was Fannie Mae was turned into a GSA which privatized profits while at the same time eliminating the risk to shareholders.

Also, under the Housing and Urban Development Act of 1968, the Government National Mortgage Association or Ginnie Mae was split off of Fannie Mae. Unlike Fannie Mae, Ginnie Mae would remain a government organization, with the function of providing: (1) FHA-- insured mortgages, (2) Veterans Administration (VA) mortgages and (3) Farmers Home Administration (FmHA) insured mortgages. The 1968 Housing and Urban Development Act also provided that Ginnie Mae loans would have the full faith and credit of the United States government behind them. However, the Act also made clear that Fannie Mae's mortgages would not have the same guarantee. Besides being explicitly stated in the Act, it was also stated on the Fannie Mae securities themselves, and in many public communications issued by Fannie Mae. Thus, neither the certificates nor payments of principal and interest on the certificates were guaranteed by the government. Nevertheless, the public believed that Fannie Mae had: (1) an explicit guarantee by the government and (2) was chartered by Congress with a direct line of credit to the US Treasury with an 'implied guarantee' of principal and interest. What helped develop this illusion of an implied guaranteed theory and greatly enhanced the success of the GSEs were the various special treatments given to Fannie Mae by the government. The implied guarantee allowed Fannie Mae and Freddie Mac (later created in 1970) to save billions in borrowing costs, as their credit rating was very good. Estimates by the Congressional Budget Office and the Treasury Department put the figure at about $2 billion per year. # 1

In 1970 the government created the Federal Home Loan Mortgage Corporation also known as Freddie Mac, to compete with Fannie Mae and thus facilitate a more competitive secondary mortgage market. In 1989 Freddie Mac was allowed to follow in the footsteps of Fannie Mae and become a privately owned but publicly chartered corporation. The net effect was that Freddie Mac like Fannie Mae became a GSEs which meant both companies were privatized for profits while at the same eliminating the risk to shareholders.

Another piece of the **"Perfect Storm"** was put in place with the passage of the HUD Reform Act in 2004, that eliminated the 2000 HUD rule, which disallowed risky high-cost loans from being credited toward affordable housing goals. So much for the **"cleans hands doctrine",** Congress was now encouraging the GSE to acquire high risk loans. The significance of HUD dropping the anti-predatory lending rules on high-risk loans in 2004 was the GSEs could now lower their standards and buy more subprime loans that would expand the housing market. As the housing market expanded during this time frame new pure subprime companies like New Century and Ameriquest entered the financial market. In 2005, as a result of the 2004 HUD ruling and the loss of market share to the new subprime companies Fannie Mae concluded it should begin guaranteeing subprime or non-conforming residential mortgages. This conclusion resulted in Fannie Mae and Freddie Macs pooling and selling high risk MBS as securities which helped expand the secondary market for those loans, which in turn expanded the housing market even more. # 2

Another contributing factor that was already mentioned was the HUD goal for Fannie and Freddie to finance more low-income and moderate-income mortgages. In 1992 the goal was set at 30% and in 2007 the goal was increased to 55%. The assumption was that Fannie

Mae's enforcement of their underwriting standards they maintained for conforming mortgages would also provide a safe and stable environment for lending to buyers who had subprime credit. The enforcement of these underwriting requirements by Fannie Mae drove business into the arms of the private mortgage lenders. The problem was many lenders aggressively marketed products to subprime borrowers without regard to future consequences. Additionally, Community Reinvestment Act regulators, under the direction of HUD's secretary Andrew Cuomo, gave higher ratings to banks that financed home loans to "credit-deprived" areas. **In essence, banks were rewarded for by-passing loan standards, and instead, approved loans to those who were at a high risk of defaulting. If banks did not adhere to these rules, then the CRA regulators limited their ability to lend.** The net result was the **"cleans hands doctrine"** no longer applied and banks were forced into making high risk loans.

Adding to the HUD pressure applied to Fannie and Freddie was the activities of private mortgage lenders. Many of the private lenders were willing to make loans to any low-income person who wanted one; thus, making it more difficult for the GSEs to even meet their 1992 30% HUD requirement let alone the 2007 goal of 55%. These private lenders also pressed the GSEs to ease credit requirements on the mortgages the GSEs were willing to purchase, so the lending institutions could qualify subprime borrowers at interest rates higher than conventional loans. Because the GSEs underwriting requirements were higher than the private mortgage lenders it became even harder for the GSEs to reach HUD's lending goal. However, in 2004 when HUD allowed the GSEs to count the purchases of subprime securities as part of their housing lending goal, these triple-A-tranches provided an easy way to meet HUD's increased requirement of 55% in 2007. Closely associated with the direct pressure from the private mortgage lenders was the indirect pressure or **"Fear"** of losing market share. This fear occurred because subprime mortgage originators had lowered their lending standards below those of the GSE's and the subprime mortgage originators could sell these subprime loans directly to Wall Street. The fear that the private lenders would dominate the market caused the GSEs to loosen their business underwriting standards in order to compete. In 2003, Fannie Mae's estimated market share for bonds backed by single-family housing was 45 percent. Just one year later, it dropped to 23.5 percent. # 3 Adding to this fear of losing market share was pressure from GSEs shareholders. These combined pressures for record profits and volume led to GSEs securitizing loans that would not have normally been securitized into mortgage back securities. Thus, the pressures on the GSEs contributed to the GSE's acquiring more subprime loans in three ways: (1) HUD increasing the required amount of subprime loans the GSEs had to purchase, (2) the **"Fear"** of not being competitive against private mortgage lenders and thus lowering their underwriting standards in order to compete, and (3) having to the meet the needs of their shareholders for more loan volume and profits. Had the GSEs remained under government ownership this last pressure would have never existed.

In 1999, The New York Times reported that Fannie Mae's move towards the subprime market: "…is taking on significantly more risk, which may not pose any difficulties during flush economic times. But the government-subsidized corporation may run into trouble in an economic downturn, prompting a government rescue similar to that of the savings and loan industry in the 1980's." # 4 Alan Greenspan stated in his testimony before the House and Senate Banking Committee in 2004, the markets believed that the U.S. government would never allow Fannie Mae or Freddie Mac to fail—as history has shown the markets were right. # 5

In hindsight it becomes apparent the creation of the GSEs and the new requirements placed on them by Congress and HUD in the **Congressional Legislative Acts** played a major factor in creating the housing and financial crisis. As a result of the housing crisis which came about because of the Financial Crisis the Federal government disbursed **$31,303,277,316** in grants to bail out homeowners. The housing grants under the TARP program were never to be paid back. The question is, was this the right thing to do?

In evaluating the causes of the financial crisis one can make an argument that forgiving the $31 billion from TARP was the right thing to do. As a result of the passage of the Congressional Legislative acts, an argument was made that the foundation to the Crisis was an attempt by HUD and Congress at social engineering home ownership for the "under-served or poor population". As mentioned, there was greed on the part of Main Street and Wall Street—but no one on Wall Street went to jail. Wall Street paid $275 billion in fines from 2002-2019 for their fraudulent practices and illegal conduct and was told not to do it again. On the other hand, banks did not want to make loans to people who could not afford to pay for them so Congress passed laws that created tools for companies like New Century Financial Corp or Countrywide that allowed for subprime and predatory lending practices to develop. It is clear that "Joe Sixpack" and the "under-served or poor population" along with Wall Street and even HUD (when it required the GSEs to purchase up to 55% of their loans from the subprime market) got caught up in the culture of financial irresponsibility. As it turned out Wall Street became the collateral beneficiary as described by Ted Truman. Ted Truman was an American economist specializing in international financial institutions and said it was impossible to design an effective rescue program to solve a financial crisis without creating some moral hazard--**"collateral beneficiaries".** "Joe Sixpack" with the grants for affordable housing under TARP and Wall Street and their executives became the **"collateral beneficiaries"** under the TARP bailout.

CHAPTER 2:
THE SOLUTION

A key element of leadership is the ability for a leader to see the correct path to take and then have the guts and the ability to build support for the direction that needs to be followed. President Richard Nixon once said: "Leaders should lead and not just follow uninformed public opinion. It is their responsibility to educate the people and the Congress about where our vital interests are and then gain support for whatever military actions (in this case domestic policy) may be necessary…." # 1

With TARP, Bush, like Nixon, refused to follow uninformed public opinion—instead he assigned the best qualified members of his administration to educate not only himself, but Congress and the American people about the problems associated with the Financial Crisis as well as building support for the correct path that was needed. The qualified members were: --Secretary of the Treasury Hank Paulson, SEC Chairman Chris Cox, and Federal Reserve Board Chairman Ben Bernanke, later FDIC Chair (from 2006-2011) Sheila Bair got involved. Bush's Nixonian leadership approach was made clear when he said: "We don't have time to worry about politics…." "Let's figure out the right thing to do and do it. I had made up my mind: The U.S. government was going all in." # 2

Under President George W. Bush, the solutions to the Financial Crisis came in two parts: the first part was developed by Treasury Secretary Hank Paulson and SEC Chairman Chris Cox. The second part of the solution was directed by the Chairman of the Federal Reserve Ben Bernanke who worked closely with Treasury Secretary Paulson. Under President Obama, Bernanke also worked with the new "gang of three" as he continued the partnership between the new Treasury Secretary, Timothy Geithner and Mary Schapiro who became Chair of the SEC in January 2009.

The Federal Reserve was the key component of the Bush "all-in policy." The unofficial partnership that developed between the Federal Reserve and Treasury was the key to bring the economy back to normal. The two institutions were intertwined in both the Bush and Obama administrations in different ways, each playing a key role in providing support to the other. Both institutions provided different types of liquidity, financial guarantees and support that led to the creation of more jobs and brought back faith and stability in the credit and housing markets which in turn led to the country having faith in the economy.

The first part of the program, as explained, was carried out mostly by the Treasury Department under the Emergency Economic Stabilization Act (EESA). The EESA granted the Secretary of the Treasury under TARP to either purchase or insure up to $700 billion in troubled assets owned by financial institutions. The goal of the EESA was to have TARP stabilize the financial markets by cleaning up the bank's balance sheets thus alleviating the widespread uncertainty and suspicion which would help provide **liquidity to the markets** in the U.S. and the world economies. Some didn't believe the financial institutions were in danger of defaulting, others wanted to let the free market take its course. Still others were concerned about spending taxpayer dollars to make up for the bad judgements of the banks. Congress at first rejected the TARP program but quickly came around after the stock market dropped 777.68 points the day after Congress had rejected the program. This was the largest point drop in market history. As a result of the stock market dropping Congress passed the EESA of 2008 and supported the TARP program. To pay for TARP Congress raised the debt ceiling to $11.3 trillion. President George W. Bush signed the EESA into law on October 3, 2008. By law the TARP program would expire two years after its inception—October 3, 2010. However, in July 2010, Treasury's authority under TARP was reduced from $700 billion to $475 billion under the Dodd-Frank Wall Street Reform and Consumer Protection Act.

Although TARP and the EESA prevented the fatal heart attack the economy was moving towards, they did create what Ted Truman called "collateral beneficiaries". The moral hazards created by Truman's "collateral beneficiaries" has been the major criticism of TARP and the EESA programs. According to former Secretary Treasury Timothy Geithner, if society wants an effective emergency program to solve a financial crisis there will be "collateral beneficiaries"—there is no way around it. # 3

Paulson said on October 15, 2008, on ABC's "Good Morning America" that he initially opposed this type of government intervention into the banking industry but that new facts and circumstances in recent days changed his mind.

Paulson's initial proposal under TARP was to purchase some of the mortgage-related toxic assets owned by the banks. Because of the complexity of the MBSs, CDOs and the CDSs ** along with the pushback from the marketplace on the value of these assists this approach was unworkable. The MBSs, CDOs and the CDSs were so complicated that, as discussed with Jupiter High-Grade CDO V mortgage bond, only a few people could understand them. The general public thinks the Federal Government has all the answers--- well it doesn't. As mentioned in the 2008 October meeting in South Carolina with President Bush, it was obvious they didn't have all the answers. It takes time to understand the problems facing the country and time to figure out which is the correct direction or path the government should follow. The EESA granted very broad authority to the Secretary of the Treasury. The reason the Secretary of the Treasury was given so much authority was the Federal Government needed flexibility to move in different directions in a timely fashion in order to handle a wide variety of economic problems associated with the Financial Crisis. # 4

As a result of the economic complexities facing the country TARP was later expanded into **five** programs: (1) banking, (2) credit, (3), the insurance industry (4) automotive industry and (5). housing.

** Credit default swaps or CDSs were financial derivative that allowed an investor to swap or offset their credit risk with that of another investor. To swap the risk of default, the lender would buy a CDS from another investor who agrees to reimburse them if the borrower defaults. Premium payments were due on a regular basis like an insurance policy.

Section 1

The Banking and Investment Programs (BIP)

The Treasury reacted quickly after the passage of TARP under the EESA as it announced its first program called the **Banking Investment Programs (BIP).** Without a viable and stable banking system in place to provide lending, the economy would probably have frozen and the financial crisis might have spiraled further out of control to a replay of the 1929 depression. Based on market conditions at the time, it became clear that financial institutions needed additional capital to absorb losses and restart the flow of credit to businesses and consumers.

On October 14, 2008, the Treasury Department committed $250 billion of the original $700 billion in TARP funds to launch its **Banking Investment Programs (BIP).** The BIP was the first of the original TARP programs created; and the BIP created an **additional 5 banking programs to deal with banking issues**. Each of these programs was established to accomplish different goals as part of the overall effort to provide liquidity and stabilize America's banking system.

The first of the five programs under the BIP was the Capital Purchase Program (CPP). The CPP was established to stabilize the financial system. As mentioned, the TARP program was initially created to primarily focus on the purchase of mortgage-backed securities and home loans. However, the CPP did not purchase the toxic mortgage-backed securities as originally planned, instead within two weeks of enactment, the CPP shifted its focus to the "preferred stock model". The Treasury started the "preferred stock model" by requiring eight of the biggest banking institutions in the country to sell preferred stock to the CPP. The eight banks were: Bank of America/Merrill Lynch, Bank of New York Mellon, Citigroup, Goldman Sachs, J.P. Morgan, Morgan Stanley, State Street, and Wells Fargo). All 8 banks were required to participate so as not to indicate that some banks were weaker than others. On October 29, 2008, the 8 financial institutions received their funds from the CPP for the sale of their preferred stock.

The CPP ultimately made 738 loans to provide capital to 709 financial institutions across the 48 states. The committed $250 billion was later reduced to $218 billion in March 2009 and by the end of the program in 2010 the CPP had disbursed $204.89 billion. The program required banks to give the government a 5% dividend on the bank stock they held that would increase to 9% in 2013. The purpose was not only to protect the taxpayers, but to encourage banks to buy back their stock within five years. Hank Paulson, then Secretary of the Treasury, knew the government would make a profit from the stocks once the economy began to grow again. In its July 2021 report the Congressional Budget Office (CBO) reported that there was just one bank out of the 709 financial institutions that still owed the CPP. The amount owed was $12,063,000 million. The Bank is One United Bank in Boston, Massachusetts which is the largest black owned bank in the country.

By August 2021, Treasury had collected **$226,780,000,000** from the CPP which included the original **$204.89 billion** plus a net gain to the TARP of **$21.89 billion** in the form of dividends, interest, and capital gains. Because the Treasury will continue to try and recover additional funds owed to the CPP this figure will probably change. # 1

In January of 2009, the Asset Guarantee Program (AGP) was the **second program** under the **BIP** to be created. The AGP was a joint program with the Treasury, the Federal Reserve, and Sheila Bair and the FDIC. The AGP supported the value of certain assets held by two financial institutions—Bank of America and Citigroup, whose failure would have caused serious harm to the financial system and the broader economy. In

January 2009, an agreement was made in principle for the government agencies to share losses on a $118 billion pool of financial instruments owned by Bank of America. Had the agreements been finalized, Treasury and the FDIC would have received preferred stock and warrants as a premium for the guarantee. But in May 2009 Bank of America decided to terminate the agreement and pay a termination fee of $425 million to the government, **$276 million** of which went to the Treasury while **$149** million went to the Federal Reserve—a net gain to the American taxpayer. No TARP or Federal Reserve funds were ever used. # 2

Also in January 2009, Citigroup followed Bank of America's lead and entered into a similar agreement with the Treasury and the FDIC to cover its potential losses of $301 billion. As a premium for the guarantee, Treasury and the FDIC received $7.1 billion of Citigroup preferred stock. Treasury also received warrants to purchase 66.5 million shares of Citigroup common stock. Like Bank of America, Citigroup requested termination of the agreement in December 2009, but the government retained a total of $5.3 billion of the $7.1 billion of preferred stock.

Since Citigroup made no claims for payments to the government, and the Treasury made no guaranteed payments of TARP funds to Citigroup, all payments received to date and the income received from the sale of the securities described above have constituted a net profit to taxpayers. The profit for the U.S. Treasury from Citigroup was **$3,850,029,313**, when adding that to the **$276 million** from Bank of America's participation in the AGP the Treasury earned **$4,126,029,313** dollars in positive returns for taxpayers. At the same time the Federal Reserve earned **$149 million** for the taxpayers.

The **third program** under the BIP had two components, the first was called**: Supervisory Capital Assessment Program (SCAP) and the second was the Capital Assistance Program (CAP)**: These programs were established to ensure that our major banking institutions had adequate capital buffers to withstand losses and meet the credit needs of their customers in a severe recession.

The SCAP was a "stress test" of the nation's 19 largest banks to determine the health of each institution. The tests were conducted in early 2009 and the results were made public, thus they helped to reduce uncertainty and restore confidence in our financial institutions. Eighteen of the 19 participating banks were found to have adequate capital buffers. Following the release of the stress test results, banks were able to raise hundreds of billions of dollars in private capital.

The CAP was established to provide additional assistance to any of those banks that were found to need financial support but could not raise adequate private capital. Eighteen of the 19 participating banks were found to have adequate capital buffers and therefore did not require any funding under CAP. CAP closed on November 9, 2009, **without making any investments or using any TARP funds.**

The **4th program** under **BIP** was the: **Targeted Investment Program (TIP):** The TIP program was created in December 2008 and gave the Treasury the necessary flexibility to provide additional or new funding to financial institutions that were critical to the functioning of the financial system. Under **TIP**, the Treasury purchased $20 billion in preferred stock from Bank of America and Citigroup Inc. In December 2009 Bank of America and Citigroup paid **$4,450,469,972** to the Treasury which included the original $40 billion from the TIP and additional **$3 billion** in dividends plus warrants from each bank. The warrants produced around **$1.4 billion** in gains thus creating a **$4,450,469,972** profit for the Treasury. # 3

The **5th and final component** under **BIP's** attempt to stabilize the America banking system was the **Community Development Capital Initiative (CDCI):** The **CDCI** program was created on February 3, 2010, to help low and moderate-income and minority communities that are underserved by traditional banks and financial services providers. The **CDCI** was created as a tool to funnel funds from the Treasury into the Community Development Financial Institution Fund which provides responsible and affordable lending to low-wealth communities. The Treasury completed funding under the **CDCI** in September 2010. Eighty-five institutions received investments totaling approximately **$570 million. The program lost $70 million as only $500 million was paid back.** # 4

Section 2
Credit Markets

The **second phase** of **TARP's** five-part program was to restore the **Credit Markets**. When the Obama Administration took office, credit markets were all but frozen, meaning that it was extremely difficult for consumers and businesses to get loans. Availability of credit is critical for small businesses to get loans, and for consumers to pay their daily bills—food, home and car loans etc. Therefore, the Federal Government took action to jumpstart these crucial markets. Twenty-seven billion was originally suggested to restart credit markets, but the total TARP funds disbursed for the Credit Market programs was $19,093,293,391 billion, **but only $18,993,293,481 were used.**

There were three **Credit Market** programs: (1) **The Public-Private Investment Program (PPIP)**, (2) **the Term Asset-Backed Securities Loan Facility (TALF) and** (3) **the SBA 7 (a) Securities Purchase Program**. Although the specific goals and implementation methods of each program differed, **the overall goal of these three programs was the same—to restart the flow of credit to meet the critical needs of small businesses and consumers.**

On March 23, 2009, the "gang of three" announced plans for two complementary federal programs (the Legacy Loans Program and the Legacy Securities Program) under the **Public-Private Investment Program** (PPIP). At the same time a second component of the Legacy Securities Program was created under TALF. These programs were designed to jump-start bank lending and securitization markets through a unique public-private partnership and committed up to $100 billion in TARP money to fund the programs. Under TALF the Federal Reserve Bank of New York authorized up to $200 billion of non-recourse loans.

The goal of the **Public-Private Investment Program** or PPIP as it was called was to **cleanse the balance sheets of U.S. banks of toxic assets like mortgage-backed securities (MBS) and restart the market for these assets, which made up the bulk of U.S. banks assets.** The PPIP is a great example of Truman's "collateral beneficiaries" paradigm. Under PPIP there were two primary programs, the Legacy Loans Program and the Legacy Securities Program.

The **Legacy Loans Program** would have used public financing from TARP to help **private entities purchase** pools of bank loan assets. The assets to be purchased created uncertainty around the balance sheets of these financial institutions, compromising their ability to raise capital and their ability to lend to business and the general consumer. Under the program: (1) the FDIC was charged with guaranteeing the loans once they were sold, (2) the Treasury provided half of the initial financing required to purchase the loans from the banks, and (3) banks would determine the loans they considered distressed and put these loans up for auction to other private market participants. (4) The FDIC would determine the eligibility of the proposed loans, and (5) the FDIC would then specify what amount they would allow for the initial purchase of the loans. (6) The maximum potential leverage or loan to value was 6 to 1. For example, if a pool of loan assets costs $42, **an initial investment of equity would be $6 leaving** $36 in debt to finance. The bidder that won the auction would be allowed to draw on the public-private investment funds from the Treasury for $3. The bidder/buyer would then be required to provide the other $3 for its half of the equity cost. (7) The buyer would then obtain financing to fund the remaining $36 that would be guaranteed by the FDIC. (8) The FDIC was then charged with managing and overseeing the servicing of the debt. (9) All loans were nonrecourse and secured only by the assets they were used to purchase.

Despite months of FDIC attempts to develop the program, it was NEVER implemented. Following its announcement, the program was criticized by some in the media and academic community as an example of "collateral beneficiaries" because they believed it would benefit private investors at the expense of the general public.

The **Legacy Securities Program** was established because private markets were hesitant to invest in legacy securities. The toxic assets or legacy securities as they are now often referred to are: (i.e., non-agency residential mortgage-Backed securities (RMBS) and commercial mortgage-backed securities (CMBS). U.S. banks owned roughly between $1-2 trillion of these compromised assets, depending how they were evaluated. The value of the toxic assets was so uncertain that there were reasonable grounds for arguing that the average asset's face value was worth anywhere from 30-60 cents on each dollar. This was one of the big uncertainties Bush brought up in the October 2008 South Carolina meeting----where do you start and how do you deal with this problem? Thus, the Legacy Securities Program was established with two primary goals in mind: (1) to create new demand for troubled mortgage-related assets, thus enabling financial institutions to sell them and (2) the Treasury wanted a considerable portion of new demand to be from private investors. The Program would accomplish this by providing: (1) government equity co-investment loans and (2) attractive public financing to those investors.

To begin the **Legacy Securities Program**: (1) the Treasury conducted an application process, which resulted in it choosing nine private sector firms (fund managers) with which to form investment partnerships—**PPIPs**. (2) Each fund manager was obliged to raise no less than $500 million in private capital during the ensuing twelve weeks—at least $20 million of which had to be supplied by its own firm. (3) Each fund manager was given responsibility over its **own PPIP**, which served as the **conduit through** which it purchased and held onto eligible securities. (4) After raising capital from the private sector, receiving matching Treasury equity, and selecting one of two debt-financing schemes made available by the Treasury, the PPIPs began to invest in mortgage securities. (5) By restarting the market for those securities, the program helped financial institutions begin to remove these assets from their balance sheets, allowing those institutions to re-deploy capital and extend credit to households and businesses.

The PPIP was designed around 3 basic principles: (1) **Maximizing the impact** of each taxpayer dollar: by using government financing **in partnership with FDIC and the Federal Reserve** who would **co-invest with private sector investors**, (2) **Shared risk** and profits with private sector participants as the program ensured that private sector participates invest alongside the taxpayer, with the private sector investors along with the taxpayers standing to lose their entire investments on a downside scenario, and (3) **the free market approach** of private investors determining the value of eligible assets, thereby reduce the likelihood that the government would overpay for these assets.

The PPIP was designed originally by the "gang of 3"as an eight-year program when it was started on March 3, 2009, but ended on September 30, 2014, when the Treasury fully recovered its TARP funds. Under the program, the Treasury originally obligated $21.9 billion of TARP funds from the PPIPs to purchase eligible assets from 9 recipients. The PPIP only invested **$18,625,147,939** of the $21.9 Billion. The PPIP produced **$22,466,407,939** which included the original **$18,625,147,939** plus net profit for the Treasury and the taxpayers of **$3,841.260,000.** #1

As mentioned, the **Term Asset Backed Loan Facility (TALF)** was launched on March 3, 2009, under section 13(3) of the Federal Reserve Act, as a dual program including both the **Federal Reserve Bank of New York (FRBNY) and the U.S. Treasury.** Under TALF the Federal Reserve Bank of New York authorized up to $200 billion of loans on non-recourse basis to holders of certain AAA-rated asset-backed securities (ABS) that were collateralized by student loans, auto loans, credit card loans, and loans guaranteed by the Small Business Administration. # 2 Yet, the program closed after only funding the purchase of $43 billion in loans. Under the TALF program: (1) The TALF money was not to go directly to businesses and consumers, but to the financial institutions who issued the asset-backed securities (ABS), (2) The FRBNY would take the securities as collateral for more loans the financial institutions might make against the ABSs, (3) To manage the TALF loans, the FRBNY was to create a special-purpose vehicle (SPV) that would buy the ABSs securing the TALF loans and (4) TARP would finance the first $20 billion of ABSs purchased for the SPV by buying debt in the SPV.

The Eligible collateral could only be U.S. dollar-denominated cash ABSs with a long-term credit rating in the highest investment-grade rating category from two or more major nationally recognized statistical rating organizations.

The U.S. economy had ground to a virtual standstill during the early months of the financial crisis. Under TALF, the "gang of 3" worked as a team with a goal of creating liquidity for the banks that were designed to boost public confidence and spending.

As the crisis developed, one of TALF's primary goals was to **add liquidity** to the economy to compensate for the market's contraction and stabilize the financial system. Under TALF, the FRBNY made non-recourse loans to buyers of AAA-rated ABS that were collateralized by loans to autos, credit cards, student loans, commercial mortgages and small businesses. It did this by giving credit protection to the banks against potential losses on TALF loans issued to banks by the FRBNY. The FRBNY gave no guarantees on the performance of the ABS's. To receive a TALF loan, Wall Street investors had to buy an ABS and pledge it as collateral against the requested TALF loan. The investors had to keep a "first loan" position—meaning that if the underlying loans performed badly, the TALF investors would lose their entire investment before the FRBNY, the U.S. Treasury or taxpayer suffered any losses. If on the other hand TALF was successful, which it was, then ABS values would increase, investors would see gains in their ABS investments as a result of the risk they took. The idea was to boost the secondary market for a number of different asset classes, such as credit cards, auto, student and Small Business Administration loans as well as commercial mortgages.

In early 2009, Treasury Secretary Geithner said he might devote up to $100 billion of TARP funds to back any losses that the Federal Reserve Bank of New York might incur under TALF, which he said would lend up to $1 trillion in Fed loans. Because of the success of TALF and the liquidity it created within the economy; in early April, Treasury officials lowered their original pledge of credit protection to $30 billion and by July of 2010, Treasury had reduced the guarantee on outstanding loans to $4.3 billion. The Fed lent a total of $71.1 billion, **but never had more than $49 billion outstanding** at one time. The TALF loan program ended on June 30, 2010, but the loans that were still outstanding to financial institutions would still have guaranteed credit protection. By June of 2012, the amount of credit protection was reduced again to $1.4 billion, because TALF had not experienced any losses and any recourse to TARP funds seemed unlikely. In January 2013, Treasury announced it had incurred no losses to TARP from TALF and that its participation in TALF was ending. The Program had made a profit of **$749,307,823.** Of the **$749,307,823** profit, $647,377,041 went to the Treasury and the balance of **$74,930,872** was a profit for the Federal Reserve. # 2

All of the TALF loans were repaid in full to the FRBNY by October 2014. The original TALF loans were scheduled to mature on March 30, 2015. The early payoff of TALF loans were a result of FRBNY 's structuring of the interest payments. The FRBNY set the loan rates lower than rates prevailing during the crisis, but above rates that would be found during normal market conditions. In setting these rates, TALF offered rates that were sufficient to attract investors back to a market that had come to a virtual halt. But as the markets recovered, investors found the TALF loan rates to be expensive, which provided an incentive for TALF borrowers to start prepaying their loans before their respective maturity dates.

The success of the TALF program is found in the number of loans issued. The TALF supported the issuance of nearly 3 million auto loans, more than 1 million student loans, nearly 900,000 loans to small businesses, 150,000 other business loans, and millions of credit card loans.

Although the TARP and the "gang of 3's" actions were criticized by many, it was not the first government bailout of the American economy and banking system.

The first government bailout of the American economy occurred under Treasury Secretary Alexander Hamilton during the financial crisis and Panic of 1792. Hamilton received notice that the banks of Maryland and New York were in financial trouble. He was also aware that a number of speculators who borrowed money from the Bank of the United States to buy stock in the Bank had defaulted on their loans. From December 29 to March 9, 1792, cash reserves in the Bank of the U.S. decreased by 34% prompting the Bank to deny renewal of nearly 25% of their outstanding 30-day loans. In order to pay off their 30-day loans many borrowers had to sell securities they had purchased, prompting the nation's first financial panic and stock market crash. Hamilton's main concern was maintaining the stability of the U.S. financial system. Like the 2007-2008 Financial Crisis, **liquidity** for financial institutions was key to keeping the economy stable. **Much like the "gang of 3" under the TALF program which had created a special-purpose vehicle (SPV) that would buy the assets securing the TALF loans, Hamilton made use of the Sink Fund of 1790 * which allowed the Federal Government to purchase open-market securities to boost liquidity and credit.** The Sink Fund was meant to assure investors and the public that the new government was committed to redeeming its debts. *

* The Funding Act of 1790 was passed to address the issue of funding the domestic debt of $21.5 million incurred by the state governments: first as Thirteen Colonies, then as states in rebellion, next as independence states in a separate nation, and then as states in a Confederation and as members of a federal Union. Through the new Department of the Treasury, the U.S. government issued U.S. Treasury Securities backed by the "full faith and credit" of the United States government and offered them to the bondholders (individual entities that held the debt of each state) of each of the former states.

The Sink Fund was controlled by a commission of 5 which included: (1) Vice President John Adams, (2) Sec. of State Thomas Jefferson, (3)

Chief Justice John Jay, (4) Attorney General Edmund Randolph and (5) Sec. of the Treasury Alexander Hamilton.

Like the TALF program, Hamilton's program provided **liquidity** to banks with hundreds of thousands of dollars to make open-market purchases of securities; as a result, the market stabilized by May 1792. Hamilton encouraged the Banks to make loans collateralized by government securities, but to lend at seven percent interest instead of six. Hamilton felt that lending at a penalty rate preserved the incentive for borrowers to obtain market funding when it was available rather than seeking recourse from the government. **During the Financial Crisis the "gang of 3" followed Hamilton's approach and charged higher interest rates to protect taxpayer**s.

Also, like Hamilton, TALF gave credit protection to banks against potential losses on loans. Hamilton also encouraged the banks to continue offering loans collateralized by US debt securities. For example, he promised the Bank of New York that the US Treasury would buy back from the Bank up to $500,000 of securities should they get stuck with excessive collateral.

By exerting his power as Secretary of Treasury and persuading a number of banks to continue offering credit throughout the crisis, Hamilton was able to limit the amount of Federal debt purchases by the Sinking Fund Commission to $243,000. Hamilton was thus able to stabilize the securities market and prevent the panic from inducing a recession.

The pattern of every financial panic that has occurred over the past two hundred years has followed the outline that occurred in the Panic of 1792: the wild speculation, the financial frenzy, the collapse that followed, and the intervention of the government as the lender of last resort to keep the rot from spreading. As described by Galbraith, the cycles of euphoria and panic are repeated as the lessons of history are ignored despite everything the Federal Reserve, Congress, the President, Stock Exchanges and other agencies may do. As said before, speculators as a species will never die.

The final effort by TARP to restore the **Credit Markets for small business** was **SBA 7 (a) Securities Purchase Program.** The Treasury launched this program to purchase up to $1 billion of securities that were guaranteed by the Small Business Administration. The loans provided additional liquidity to the markets to increase overall small business lending. Securities purchased by the Treasury included approximately 700 loans across 17 diverse industries including retail, food services, manufacturing, scientific and technical services, health care, and educational services.

No new loans were made after October 3, 2010, when the TARP's authority to make new purchases in existing programs expired, the Treasury had purchased $368,145,452 of securities that were guaranteed by the Small Business Administration. By January 24, 2012, Treasury had closed the SBA7 Program; the Program and had sold all the securities and recovered its original investment of **$368,145,452** plus a profit of **$8,602,850.**

Section 3

American International Group (AIG)

The threat of the failure of **AIG** or **American International Group** resulted in the **third** leg of the TARP program. Under the program the **U.S. Treasury and the Federal Reserve Bank of New York (FRBNY)** committed a combined total of $180.34 billion to stabilize the company. According to the Treasury's report as of December 31, 2008, Treasury had purchased $40 billion in preferred shares from AIG through TARP and later extended a $29.8 billion line of credit for a total commitment of $69.84 billion. AIG later only drew down $27.8 billion of the line of credit and the remaining $2 billion obligation was canceled thus, making TARP's total commitment to AIG $67.84 billion. The Federal Reserve provided the balance of $112.5 billion for a final total of $180.34 billion. # 1

At the height of the financial crisis in September 2008, AIG was on the brink of failure. At the time, AIG was the largest provider of conventional insurance in the world. The company insured 76 million customers in approximately 140 countries with more than 30 million customers in the United States. Most of its business was in general life, auto, home, business, and travel insurance, as well as retirement products like fixed and variable annuities, including municipal bonds. Illustrating the danger of an AIG bankruptcy, a September 17, 2008, CNN Money article (Why the Fed pulled the trigger on AIG) stated an AIG failure was more serious than Lehman Brothers. If AIG's assets hit the market all at once there wouldn't be enough qualified buyers to digest the company and its subsidiaries which would likely cause worldwide chaos and send values on commercial paper plummeting. Consequently, there was a need to create another "collateral beneficiary" program.

AIG's problems started when it sold credit protection through its London unit in the form of credit default swaps **(SDSs is a contract whereby a buyer of a bond attempts to eliminate a possible loss from a default on the bond by getting insurance on the bond it case it fails)** on collateralized debt obligations (CDOs). By 2008 when the financial markets were declining AIG's Financial Products division had already entered into credit default swaps (a new economic tool) to insure **$441 billion worth of securities originally rated AAA. Of those securities about 13% or $57.8 billion were structured debt securities backed by subprime loans.** When the Credit Rating Agencies downgraded AIG's credit rating the company was required to post additional collateral with its trading counterparties, leading to a liquidity crisis that began on September 16, 2008, and essentially bankrupted AIG.

Because of the domestic and global impacts and because there were no other qualified buyers who could digest the company or bridge the financial gap created by the AIG problem, the Federal Government under the leadership of President George W. Bush had to step up to the plate--there was no choice. **The only problem with the bailout was that there was no restriction on AIG executive bonuses**. In March 2009, AIG compounded public cynicism concerning "too big to fail" when it announced that it would pay $165 million in executive bonuses. The bonuses were justified by AIG as retention bonuses—not merit bonuses. The AIG executives are an example of "collateral beneficiaries" who were asked to stay and safely unwind the CDSs whose markets had disappeared. **These derivatives were time sensitive and so complicated that no one else could understand them.** It was argued that letting these swaps fall apart would have cost the Treasury more than $165 million. The questions are: (1) would the executives really have walked from their jobs, (2) were the bonuses really needed to keep them on the job, or (3) would the threat of a possible prosecution be enough to keep them on the job.

The Treasury, the FRBNY and AIG completed a restructuring plan for AIG that enabled the company to be restored to financial stability and fully repay taxpayers. Since the financial crisis the size of AIG has been cut nearly in half as it sold non-core assets.

According to the U.S. Department of the Treasury, in December 2012 it sold its remaining shares of AIG common stock ($51.6 billion) and preferred stock ($23.2 billion) which concluded its financial relationship with AIG. Thus, the positive effect of the stabilizing efforts from both TARP and the Federal Reserve was a return of **$203,065,967,492** from the AIG investment. Out of the **$203,065,967,492** that was returned from the original investment of **$180,340,000,000** from both TARP and the Federal Reserve. TARP realized a **$5,025,967,492** profit, after expenses from its original $67.84 billion investment. The Federal Reserve collected **$130,200,000,000** from its investment of $112.5 billion in AIG which included a profit of **$17.7 billion.** The positive effect also included the billions that were saved domestically in municipal bond markets, and the broader economy as well as preventing a negative impact on global financial markets. # 2

Section 4

Automotive Industry Financing Program (AIFP)

The fourth part of the TARP was an investment of **$79,922,932,000** into the **Automotive Industry Financing Program (AIFP**) through 6 different programs. The programs were: $50,744,648,329 for GM, $10,748,284,222 for Chrysler, $17.2 billion for Ally Financial [formerly GMAC], $1.5 billion to Chrysler Financial, $5 billion for the Auto Supplier Support Program and $640 million for the Auto Warranty Commitment Program. The programs were launched in December 2008 to prevent the uncontrolled liquidation of General Motors (GM) and Chrysler along with the collapse of the rest of the U.S. auto industry. The potential for such a disruption posed a significant risk to the financial and economic stability of the country. According to the Center for Auto Research, if GM and Chrysler had gone under, it would have cost an estimated $39 billion to $105 billion in lost tax revenues as well as assistance to the unemployed. Plus, the government would have been on the hook for billions in promised pension payments to autoworkers. #1

The ripple effect of the collapse would have been large on the interconnected vehicle industry supply chain, touching suppliers, auto dealers, and the communities where auto-manufacturing was a major industry. This could have led to a loss of close to 900,000 American jobs in the auto-manufacturing and related industries. Instead, according to the Bureau of Labor Statistics only 334,000 jobs were lost in auto-manufacturing because of TARP. As the U.S. auto industry recovered the job losses were gradually reversed and in July 2016 the auto-manufacturing employment surpassed its pre-financial crisis level of 957,000 in December 2007.

Recognizing that both the major U.S. motor vehicle manufacturing companies and their vehicle financing companies were on the verge of collapse, the George W. Bush Administration in Decembers 2008 and January 2009 provided $24.8 billion in assistance to both GM and Chrysler as well as their finance companies--- (GM $14.3 billion, Chrysler LLC $4 billion, GMAC $5 billion and Chrysler Financial $1.5 billion). # 2

When President Obama took office, America's automobile industry was on the brink of collapse. The financial crises had nearly frozen access to credit for vehicle loans and sales had plunged by 40%. Faced with that sober reality, the Obama Administration to its credit, continued the **"all-in policy"** and moved quickly to protect the broader economy by stabilizing the industry. Under the TARP program GM received a total of $50,744,648,329 in assistance. Thirty billion of the $50.7 billion was provided during GM's bankruptcy proceedings to facilitate the restructuring of a newer and smaller GM. During GM's restructuring $16.4 billion of the $30 billion was not used and remained in an escrow account until September 30, 2009. In December 2013 the Treasury sold the balance of its shares in GM which completed its ties to GM. The Treasury recouped **$39,436,410,235** of its original $50.7 billion from the escrow account and the sales of stock in GM. The result was a **$11,308,238,094 shortfall.** # 3

Without TARP's support, GM would not have been able to pay creditors, suppliers, or workers and would most likely have entered bankruptcy earlier with a less certain outcome. TARP's support enabled GM to reorganize itself in a more orderly manner and reduced collateral damage for many auto suppliers and some of the other automakers that bought parts from them.

Under Treasury, TARP loaned $10,748,284,222 to Chrysler under an agreement that required Chrysler to implement a viable restructuring plan. In March 2009, the Obama Administration determined that the business plan submitted by Chrysler was unsatisfactory and concluded that Chrysler was not viable as a stand-alone company. The Administration determined that Chrysler could only achieve viability by partnering with the international car company Fiat. As part of the planned restructuring, in April 2009, Chrysler filed for bankruptcy protection. In May 2009, Treasury provided $1.9 billion to Chrysler under a debtor-in-possession financing agreement for assistance during its bankruptcy proceedings.

Chrysler emerged from bankruptcy in June 2009 as a newly formed entity, Chrysler Group LLC. Since then, Chrysler has lowered its structural costs, adopted new technologies, rejuvenated its product line, and rebuilt its brands.

More than **$9.5 billion of the $10.7 billion** committed to Chrysler has been returned to the Treasury through principal repayments, interest, and canceled commitments. The TARP will not recover the remaining **$1,212,849,005** outstanding investment in Chrysler.

Chrysler Financial: In January 2009, Treasury announced that it would lend up to $1.5 billion to a special purpose vehicle (SPV) created by Chrysler Financial to enable the company to finance the purchase of Chrysler vehicles and help keep the automaker out of bankruptcy protection. Chrysler Financial used only **$123,076,735** of the TARP loan to fund more than 85,000 consumer loans to support the sale of Chrysler, Jeep and Dodge vehicles for Chrysler LLC. In July 2009, Chrysler Financial fully repaid the **$123,076,735 loan along with $49,671,126 in interest.**

Ally Financial (formerly GMAC): As part of the government's assistance to the automotive industry, Treasury also invested a total of **$16,300,000,000** of TARP's funds into Ally Financial. In May 2009, GMAC Bank was rebranded as Ally Bank. The Treasury determined that without government assistance, Ally would have been forced to suspend financing lines to creditworthy dealerships, leaving them unable to purchase automobile inventory for their lots. Without orders for cars,

GM would have suffered a drop in demand and would have been forced to slow or shut down its factories indefinitely. Given GM's significant overhead, a slow-down or stoppage in production of this magnitude would probably have toppled GM.

Beginning in 2011, Ally executed a substantial restructuring plan and sold its international operations. Ally's restructuring plan proved to be successful. As of June 30, 2012, Ally Financial was the 15th largest U.S. banking holding company, with approximately $178.6 billion in total assets. Between January and December 2014, Treasury sold all of its common stock in Ally. Following the sale of its Ally stock, Treasury fully wound down its auto equity investments through TARP as well its last remaining major stake in TARP.

In total Treasury recovered **$19.38 billion** on its TARP investment in ALLY, roughly **$3.6 billion bn** more than the original **$16.3** billion investment # 4

Auto Supplier Support Program (ASSP): This program was announced in March 2009 and provided guarantees and financing for auto parts suppliers who might otherwise be unable to access credit. The suppliers could get a guarantee that they'd be paid for their parts even if the auto company they supplied went under. On April 9, 2009, the Treasury made all of the funds available: $3.5 billion for GM's parts suppliers and $1.5 billion for Chrysler's. Ultimately, only **$413,076,735** was loaned out and **$529,476735** was paid back. The U.S. Treasury made a profit of **$116,400,000**. #5

Auto Warranty Commitment Program (AWCP): The program was intended to bolster consumer confidence by alleviating a major risk to consumers (the loss of warranty benefits from GM and Chrysler) associated with the companies' potential bankruptcies. At the outset, the Treasury dedicated up to $1.1 billion for the AWCP's implementation. In the end, it extended a total of only **$640.7 million** in loans to GM and Chrysler. The program closed on July 21, 2009, without either company being required to pay warranty claims. The Treasury recouped all of the **$640.7 million** loan principal and netted a profit of **$5.5 million** in interest payments. # 6

Section: 5

The Affordable Housing Programs

After George W. Bush left office, President Obama picked up the ball on the "all-in policy" and continued the leadership practices and vision that Bush had established. As a result of the housing crisis, the Treasury, under Obama launched the **Making Home Affordable Program (MHA)** in February 2009, to help struggling homeowners avoid foreclosure. The MHA helped homeowners avoid foreclosure by providing a variety of solutions under its **Home Affordable Modification Program (HAMP)** and the **Hardest Hit Fund (HHF)** program. The MHA program set new standards that helped transform the mortgage industry, resulting in more than 3.9 million private-sector mortgage modifications through October 2013.

By the time the Obama administration took office in January 2009, home prices had fallen for 30 straight months. Home values had fallen by nearly one-third. Fannie Mae and Freddie Mac had been in conservatorship for four months, and American families were struggling to keep their homes. The ratio of household debt to disposable personal income had risen from 77% in 1990 to 127% by the end of 2008. # 1

Under the HAMP program created by the MHA, homeowners had the ability to modify or refinance their home loans, get temporary forbearance if they were unemployed, or transition out of homeownership with a short sale or deed-in-Lieu of foreclosure. According to an article in CNNMoney.com on January 15th, 2009, foreclosures spiked more than 81% in 2008 with more than 3.1 million foreclosure filings issued during the year. A total of 861,664 families lost their homes in 2008. Over 1.8 million families out of over four million households who went through foreclosure during the Financial Crisis took advantage of HAMP. The program allowed creditworthy homeowners, who were "underwater" (the loan amount exceeding the current property value) in their homes, to refinance with lower mortgage rates and avoid foreclosure. Only mortgages originated on or prior to January 1, 2009, could qualify for the HAMP. The program expired on December 30, 2016.

The question is why didn't more people take advantage of HEMP? This would have pumped billions into the economy and helped those millions of homeowners avoid foreclosure. The problem was the banks. CitiMortgage and JPMorgan Chase were among the banks that refused the most HAMP claims. The banks cherry-picked applicants and refused to consider those with lower equity. This can be explained historically—during good times banking becomes a wild west show and anybody with a pulse can get a loan as was demonstrated by the events leading up to the 2007-2008 Financial Crisis. Once the free-for-all is over banks historically become very wary of risk and become overly conservative and turn down what would normally be considered a sound loan. # 2

According to the Treasury's monthly TARP report to Congress by February 28, 2022, only $21.94 billion of the $29.9 billion funds set aside for HAMP had been disbursed.

As mentioned, the MHA also established the **Hardest Hit Fund (HHF).** As part of the Obama administration's overall strategy for restoring stability to the housing market, **HHF** provided targeted aid to families through funding by state Housing Finance Agencies (HFAs) to develop locally tailored foreclosure prevention solutions in areas that had been hard hit by home price declines and high unemployment. From its initial announcement, the program evolved from a $1.5 billion initiative for the HFAs in five states which had the steepest home price declines; to a program by August 31, 2021 that had expanded to $9,503,277,316, encompassing 18 states and the District of Columbia. The Treasury partnered with the state Housing Finance Agency who would run the HHF programs, which underlined the importance of participation and partnership at the state level in each of these housing programs. Each state HFA's ability to manage the day-to-day operations of these programs allowed Treasury to focus on and manage larger and more long-term issues within and among the programs.

The affordable housing program was the final component of TARP. The program's original obligation was $32.56 billion to help prevent avoidable foreclosures and keep families in their homes. By August 31, 2021, the Treasury had disbursed **$31.4 billion** of the original $32,56 billion under TARP for the MHA. Under MHA the funds were obligated to two housing programs: the first was $22.91 billion to the **Making Home Affordable Program (HAMP)** and the second was $9.6 billion for the **Hardest Hit Fund (HHF).** The HHF was originally funded for $7.6 billion; but later in February 2016 when the MHA was extended to the end of 2020, another $2 billion was added to the project making the total of $9.6 billion for the **Hardest Hit Fund (HH**F). But as mentioned, only **$9.503 billion** was disbursed to 19 recipients. All the TARP's future disbursements for housing are expected to occur through its mortgage programs in the form of grants to borrowers. For those future payments, the estimated cost is **$.04 billion.** # 3

The Home Affordable Refinance Program (HARP) was created by the Federal Housing Finance Agency in March 2009 to allow millions of borrowers who found themselves in a difficult predicament after the U.S. housing bubble burst in 2008. As a result of the housing bubble burst many homeowners saw the value of their homes drop below the balance of their mortgage. For example, if a house was purchased for $160,000 but was worth only $100,000 the loan-to-value ratio (LTV) would be 120%. Banks traditionally require a loan-to-value ratio of 80%. If the LTV were higher the homeowner would have their refinancing request denied or be required to pay for private mortgage insurance (PMI). The required insurance could nullify the benefit of refinancing. The program was only available for mortgages that were guaranteed by either Freddie Mac or Fannie Mae (the GSEs) and applied to mortgages that were sold to either of those GSEs prior to May 31, 2009. The program was created in coordination with both Freddie Mac and Fannie Mae and the HARP was responsible for regulating them. # 4

The HAMP and the HHF programs represent another example of Truman's "collateral beneficiaries", but this time to the taxpayers. Because the funds were disbursed as grants none of the **$31.4 billion** was required to be repaid.

Another example of Truman's "collateral beneficiaries" that was passed during the Bush administration but was not a part of TARP, was the Housing and Economic Recovery Act (HERA) of July 30, 2008. HERA was a piece of legislative reform passed by Congress in response to the subprime mortgage crisis that launched a foreclosure relief program. The law allowed the Federal Housing Administration (FHA) to guarantee up to $300 billion in new 30-year fixed-rate mortgages for subprime borrowers. HERA was ultimately intended to overhaul regulations of Fannie Mae and Freddie Mac in order to renew public faith in the government-sponsored enterprises (GSEs) and to prevent the circumstances that helped lead to predatory lending and the Financial Crisis. On September 7, 2008, Fannie Mae and Freddie Mac were essentially nationalized. The companies were placed under the conservatorship of the Federal Housing Finance Agency. Under the terms of the rescue plan the Treasury invested **$191,484,000,000** in return for preferred stock. Like AIG, the investment in Fannie and Freddie turned out to be very profitable. Again, it was the actions of the "all-in policy" and the leadership of both the Bush and Obama administrations that stabilized the housing market and produced a return of **$301,006,000,000** which included a profit to the taxpayers of **$109,522,000,000.** Thus, **$109,522,000,000** by the Federal Reserve should also be added to the profit margin gained under the "all-in policy" as a result of the economic recovery.

A final TARP housing program was the **Federal Housing Administration (FHA)** Refinance program which was passed by the Obama Administration on March 26, 2010 and expired on December 31, 2012. The program was designed to be funded with $8.12 billion from the $29.9 billion TARP funds that had already been set aside for the Home Affordable Modification Program (HAMP). In March 2013, Treasury extended a letter of credit facility to guarantee funding coverage for loans refinanced throughout the eligibility period. At the same time Treasure extended the program to December 2014 but reduced the amount from $8.12 billion to $1 billion.

The program was designed to offer incentives for holders of existing single-family loans where the borrower is "underwater" to reduce the outstanding principal balance of the underwater portion of the loan, in conjunction with FHA refinancing the remaining loan balance. The homeowner must be current on the existing loan, and other FHA standards applied. A key point was the existing lender must write off at least 10% of the current outstanding loan balance. Because participation depended on financial institutions willingness to make meaningful principal reductions on their existing loans this program was not widely used. Only a few thousand loans were made under this program.

Section: 6

The Federal Reserve and the Liquidity Crisis

The guarantee program for money market mutual fund deposits was not a part of TARP, but was an important part of the "all-in policy" and the Federal Reserve's attempt to stabilize the economy.

In the U.S. there was a need to guarantee all money market mutual fund deposits. A money market mutual fund is an open-ended mutual fund that invests in short-term debt of a company's commercial paper. Money market mutual fund deposits are regarded as being as safe as bank deposits yet providing a higher yield and are important providers of liquidity to financial intermediaries. The Federal Reserve reported that for most of 2008 there was a total of $1.8 trillion in outstanding commercial paper; $763.6 billion was asset-back commercial paper (ABCP), and $975.4 billion was not backed. By December 2009, there were more than 1,700 companies in the United States that issued commercial paper: with the overwhelming majority being financial institutions. As money market funds are used to pay for day-to-day operations, (as companies borrowed against their commercial paper as they rolled over their short-term debt) any drop in demand would create a potentially liquidity crisis by preventing companies from getting funds they needed for their day-to-day operations. The vast majority (69%) of commercial paper was issued with maturities of 1-4 days. If companies cannot issue new debt to repay maturing debt, and do not have cash on hand to pay it back, they would default on their obligations and would have to file for bankruptcy. After Lehman Brothers filed for Chapter 11 bankruptcy protection on September 15, 2008, and other pending financial troubles started to unravel, Wall Street investors panicked which began an unprecedented run-on money market mutual fund account. On September 17, in a fire sale, investors withdrew or redeemed a record $144.5 billion from their money market accounts. During a typical week, only about $7 billion is withdrawn. These redemptions not only created panic and uncertainty but caused a drop in the value of the unsecured commercial paper and also a drop in demand for commercial paper itself, especially for maturities greater than overnight. Without the commercial-paper market, which finances companies like automakers, lending institutions and credit-card companies, factories would have to shut down, people would lose their jobs, and the real economy would slide into another Great Depression. **The money market mutual fund deposit crisis demonstrated one of the primary goals of the Federal Reserve's guarantee program. Which was to add liquidity to the financial system in-order to compensate for the market contraction in order to maintain the stability of the financial system and the functioning of the economy**. # 1

This abrupt withdrawal of capital from money market mutual funds, strained **market liquidity.** The strain on liquidity also occurred because banks were hoarding cash as they feared taking on bad debt and feared a possible run on their bank by corporate investors. Nobody knew who they could trust to lend to or whose balance sheet they could rely on. Normally, financial institutions have about **$2 billion** on hand at any given time. **By September 19, 2008, that number had risen to $190 billion.**

In response to this crisis on September 19, 2008, the US Department of the Treasury announced an optional program to "ensure the holdings of any publicly offered eligible money market mutual fund that pays a fee to participate in the program." The program was similar to the Federal Deposit Insurance Corporation or FDIC program that the Federal government offered individuals who had deposits in a bank. The guarantee was backed by assets of the Treasury Department's Exchange Stabilization Fund, up to a maximum of $50 billion. This program only covered assets invested in funds before September 19, 2008. The program stabilized the system by reducing the redemption crisis. The guarantee program ended on September 18, 2009, with no losses and generated **$1.2 billion** in revenue for the Federal Government and taxpayers in participation fees. Because the money market mutual fund program came about as a result of the "all-in policy" this income will be applied to the financial balance sheet under funds collected by the "all-in policy". # 2

CHAPTER 3:

The Profit /Loss and Final TARP Balance Sheet

In September 2023, the last remaining investments made by the Treasury through the TARP was repaid, thereby ending the program. The Treasury no longer holds any assets related to the program and is not authorized to make further disbursements. Consequently, the September 30, 2023, report by the CongressionalBudget Office (CBO) is their final assessment of the costs of the TARP. The total amount of funds directly disbursed by TARP under its 5 programs was $442,729,452,728. After the U.S. Treasury added its cost of $1,495,185,399 for its interest and administration expenses; the total for TARP was $444,224,638,127. # 1

It should be noted that the CBO and the OMB (Office of Management and Budget) have used similar approaches to evaluate TARP's programs for purchasing assets and making grants, however, there are differences in their final numbers. For example, OMB'S most recent estimate of TARP's cost for the Affordable Housing Programs is $31.4 billion, but the CBO's estimate for the same program and time period is $31.8 billion.

The breakdown of the FIVE programs is as follows:

(1) Five Banking Programs:	Spent	Profit/Loss for Taxpayers
[1] CCP	$204,890,000,000	$21,890,000,000
[2] AG2P -B of A / Citibank	$0	$4,126,029,313
[3] SCSP and the CAP	$0	$0
[4] TIP	$40,000,000,000	$4,450,469,972
[5] CDCI Program	$570,000,000	-$70,000,000
TARP Spent	$245,460,000,000	
Net Profit After Loans Paid		$30,396,499,285
* Spending and profit for Federal Reserve:	$0	*$149,000,000

(2) Three Credit Programs:	Spent on Program	Profit/Loss for Taxpayers:
[1] The Public-Private Investment Program or PPIP		
Legacy Loans Program	Never Implemented	$0
Legacy Securities Program	$18,625,147,939	$3,841,260,000
[2] TALF Credit Protection	No Funds Were Allocated	$647,377,041
[3] SBA 7 (a) Program	$368,145,452	$8,602,850
TARP Spending only	$18,993,293,391	
TARP Net Profit only After Loans Paid		$4,497,239,891
* Spending and Profits for the Federal Reserve	$49,000,000,000	$74,930,872

(3) The insurance industry:....................	**AIG Spent**	**Profit for Taxpayers**
TARP Spent:...................................	**$67,840,000,000**	**$5,025,967,492**
Profit After Loans Paid	**$180,340,000,000**	**$22,725,967,49**
* Spending and Profits for the Federal Reserve................	$112,500,000,000	$17,700,000,000

(4) Six Automotive Programs.....................Spent		Profit/Loss for Taxpayers
[1] General Motors	**50,744,648,329**	**-$11,308,238,094**
[2] Chrysler	**$10,748,284,222**	**-$1,212,849,005**
[3]Chrysler Financial	**$123,076,735**	**$49,671,126**
[4] Ally	**$16,300,000,000**	**$3,057,502,859**
[5] ASSP Auto Supplier Support	**$413,076,735**	**$116,400,000**
[6]AWCP Auto Warranty Program	**$640,700,000**	**$5,500,000**
TARP Spent........................	**$78,969,786,021**	
Net Loss After All Payments		**-$9,292,013,114**

(5) The Housing Programs

Total: Grants Provided to Housing Programs: -----------	**$31,465,373,316**
Estimated future cost by the CBO's as of March 2023: -----	**$1,000,000**
Total Projected for the Grants Not Repaid: ------------	**$31,466,373,316**

TARP Total: Profit/Loss After Loans Paid-- * $442,729,452,728 -$830,409,734

*Funds contributed by the Federal Reserve and the Profits made from those funds are NOT included in these final figures for TARP.

After calculating all TARP expenditures, profits and losses reported to Congress by the congressional Budget Office in their **Troubled Asset Relief Program-April 2023;** the **final cost at that time in that report was: $443,630,422,818.** # 1 The Report rounded the final figure to $444,000,000,000. Figures may not match OMB's or Treasury's figures due to their rounding in their reports, or the date of their report as new figures are continuing to be reported as more income is repaid. The most recent figures for 2024 are as mentioned above **$442,729,452,728** Most of the figures are taken from the TARP program's latest summary. Besides the actual TARP disbursements, the Treasury reported the total operating expenses for TARP was **$1,495,185,399** as of August 31, 2021. These expenses were for financial cost and legal firms who supervised the TARP. These expenses needed to be added in calculating the total cost of TARP. As mentioned, the total TARP funds allocated was **$442,729,452,728.** Adding the government operating expenses (which included interest) as reported by the U.S. Treasury of **$1,495,185,399** for the TARP, made the final total for its funding and administration cost to be **$444,224,638,127.** #1

The success of TARP was based on the unofficial partnership that GW Bush's "all-in policy" developed. Federal Reserve Board Chairman Ben Bernanke's leadership under the "gang of 3 was aggressive and very significant. No one was better suited as Fed Chief than Ben Bernanke as he had spent his academic life studying the Great Depression and financial policies applied during the Depression. Bernanke was also a student of Walter Bagehot who was an English journalist and businessman. Bagehot, in his book **Lombard Street, A Description of the Money Market** (published in 1873) became the first to articulate what a central bank should do to prevent a panic from becoming a financial crisis. Bagehot's methods were based on **2 key principles:**

1. **Central banks should lend early and freely to solvent firms against good collateral.** By doing so central banks may be able to quell powerful panic-driven demands for liquidity and their potentially negative effects on the economy. Providing a virtually unlimited source of **liquidity** to institutions can avert the fire sales that can lead to decreases in asset values, reduction in wealth, and a costly contraction in economic activity. Providing **liquidity** can also enable a continuation of lending by financial institutions that is necessary to support continued activity in the economy. **This was and is the significance of TARP, the "gang of three" and the reason behind Warren Buffett's comment on Bush.**
2. Lending only at a penalty rate preserves the incentive for borrowers to obtain market funding when it is available and avoids the creation of a moral hazard. # 2_

Under the Federal Reserve's efforts, Bernanke applied these key principles from Bagehot, but also from the lessons in history from Hamilton, and the Great Depression. Bernanke's efforts also resulted in the Federal Reserve collecting a **$128,645,930,872** profit (as shown below) for the American taxpayers. Bernanke once said: "Some people don't understand—fulfilling the responsibility as lender of last resort is what the Fed was created to do. This is what central banks have been doing for 300 years." # 3

The "all-in policy's" team effort among other things, also saved AIG and returned $112.5 billion back to the Treasury while making a profit from AIG for the Federal Reserve and taxpayers of $17.7 billion. This $17.7 billion should be added to the profit margin created by GW Bush's "all-in policy".

Another team effort between the Federal Reserve Bank of New York (FRBNY) and the U.S. Treasury under TARP was the Term Asset-Backed Securities Loan Facility program (TALF). As discussed, TALF was a funding facility under the FRBNY who issued loans with terms of up to five years to holders of eligible asset-backed securities (ABS). The

TALF was intended to assist the financial markets in accommodating the credit needs of consumers and businesses of all sizes by facilitating the issuance of ABS collateralized consumer and business loans; it was also intended to improve the market conditions for ABS financial interments. The result was another profit for the taxpayers of **$749,307,823** (90% or **$674,377,041** was a profit for TARP and the Treasury the other 10% balance of **$74,930,782** was a profit for FRBNY). Again, the Treasury portion of the profits should be added to the results of the "all-in policy".

Bernanke, and the Federal Reserve also helped stabilize the domestic economy by creating such programs as the Commercial Paper Funding facility, the Money Market Investor Funding Facility, the Asset-Backed Commercial Paper Money Market Mutual Fund Liquidity Facility and the Term Asset-Backed Securities Loan Facility. All of these programs complimented and supported the partnership between the Federal Reserve and the Treasury which created badly needed **liquidity** for the U.S. economy.

One reason the American public took longer to accept TARP and Bush's "all-in Policy" program was that the Federal Reserve under Chairman Ben Bernanke opened its vault to the world on a scope as never seen before. The Federal Reserve **pumped liquidity**, the lifeblood of credit markets, into the financial circulatory system of not only the U.S. economy, but the world economy as they both were experiencing potentially fatal heart attacks. Domestically, between March 2008 - May 2009 the Federal Reserve pumped $9 trillion of liquidity in short-term loans to 18 financial institutions. The Fed's efforts to stave off a financial crisis reached far beyond Wall Street, touching manufacturers like Detroit automakers, General Electric, and Harley-Davidson, central banks from Britain to Japan and insurers and pension funds in Sweden, South Korea and AIG—the world's largest insurance company.

In foreign markets between December 2007 - October 2008, the Federal Reserve opened its swap lines with foreign central banks, allowing them to temporarily trade their currencies for dollars to relieve pressures in their financial markets. The European Central Bank drew the most heavily on these currency arrangements. However, nine other central banks made use of the currency swaps: Australia, Denmark, England, Japan, Mexico, Norway, South Korea, Sweden and Switzerland. The **liquidity** supplied by the Federal Reserve under the "all-in policy" in both foreign and domestic markets supported money-market mutual funds, commercial paper, and short-term borrowing that companies relied on for day-to-day operations like meeting payroll and paying vendors.

If President Bush would have bowed to congressional and public opinion the country would most likely have experienced a depression equal to or greater than the Great Depression of 1929. Public and private entities alike were opposed to TRAP. The American public felt TARP was "deeply unfair" as some financial institutions got taxpayer-paid bailouts and emerged in better shape from the Financial Crisis than millions of ordinary Americans. This public attitude towards TARP is the classical downside of Ted Truman's principle of "collateral beneficiaries". What the public failed to understand is if there were no "collateral beneficiaries" there would probably have been a depression equivalent to 1929.

Besides the bailout to financial institutions, public outrage was focused on top hedge fund managers who earned more after the financial crash in 2009 than they did before in 2007 or during the crisis in 2008. The top 25 hedge fund managers earned $22.3 billion in 2007 when the economy was booming and more than $25 billion in 2009 after the financial crash. * As mentioned, the financial institutions justified these payments in order to keep their key employees who had the knowledge to unwind complex financial products like Jupiter High-Grade CDO V that were bundled into MBSs. * # 4

CHAPTER 4:
CONCLUSION

Under George W. Bush's "all-in policy" the Federal Government committed bailout money to 989 recipients. As discussed earlier, those recipients received a total of $442,730,453,718 in TARP funds from 14 different programs. If one is looking at the total amount of funds received back for the taxpayers under the Bush and Obama administrations "all in policy" as a result of the financial crisis, an argument can be made that $128 billion received by the Federal Reserve and $275 billion ($16 and $259) in fines received from financial institution for the Treasury should also be included in the profit column. Some might say this is mathematical gymnastics in an attempt to justify TARP---but if the financial crisis had not happened then the $442.7 billion would not have been spent and the $275 billion would have never been collected. **The attempt here is to look at the overall cost of the financial crisis to the treasury and the taxpayer.** # 1

A summary of profits under TARP by the Federal Reserve as a result of Bush's "all in policy" are as follows:

Under the Banking Program: Profits from AGP to the Federal Reserve: **$149,000,000**

Under the Credit Program: Profits from TALF to the Federal Reserve: **$74,930,872**

Under the AIG Insurance Program; Profits to the Federal Reserve: **$17,700,000,000**

Profits from the overhaul of Fannie and Freddie Mac: **$109,522,000,000**

Profit from the guarantee for Money Market Mutual Funds deposit: **$1,200,000,000**

Profits for the Federal Reserve ------ "all-in policy" $128,646,930,872

A summary of fines levied against financial institutions by the Federal Government between 2002-2019 are as follows:

Fines / settlement fees paid by financial institutions between 2002-2008 .... **$16,175,739,273**

Fines / settlement fees paid by financial institutions between 2009-2019.................................... **$259,203,393,285**

Total fines collected by the Treasury --------- **$275,379,132,558**

The final cost of TARP was **$442,729,452,728** additionally there were expenses of $1,495,185,399 the government incurred as a result of TARP thus, making the cost of TARP to be $444,224,638,127

When all the expenses are added and all the revenue collected by the Treasure and the Federal Reserve are included, as well as the fines paid by financial institutions the RESULT of TARP and the "all-in policy" was a

PROFIT to the American taxpayer of **$403,185,383,668** after spending **$31,503,277,316** in grants for affordable housing for those the hardest hit by the Financial Crisis.

Loss from the TARP after ALL payments: .... **-$839,679,762**

Profit made by the Federal Reserve: **$128,645,930,872**

Total fines collected by the Treasury: **$275,379,132,558**

Total Profit for the American Taxpayer **$403,185,383,668**

Also on the profit side, almost 900,000 jobs were saved in the auto industry and its supporting industries alone, as well as thousands of jobs in other businesses that provided key support to the economy. # 2

The alternative to leadership under both Presidents Bush and Obama would have been, as many have suggested, "let the free market work its magic". The question is, what would that magic be and how would it have been implemented? The free-market magic would have had to deal with the **liquidity** problem for the United States and the world as well as four major failures occurring within the United States at the same time: (1) bank and credit market failures that would lead to a lack of credit for individuals and businesses, (2) the bankruptcy of AIG, the largest insurance company in the world, (3) the failure of the auto industry which would have included the possible bankruptcy of GM and Chrysler, and (4) a housing crisis. A fifth, but underlying problem would be the unemployment factor that would be created by all the failures; and what would happen to all the people in the U.S. and world economies who were affected by the Financial Crisis?

The hostility towards the "all-in policy" came from both the left and the right. Senator Elizabeth Warren, Democrat from Massachusetts, took to the Senate floor in the closing minutes of the 113th Congress to blast the power of Wall Street: "Enough is enough, Washington already works really well for the billionaires and the big corporations and the lawyers and the lobbyists, but what about the families who lost their homes or their jobs or their retirement savings?" The problem with Senator Warren's statement is that she didn't come up with a solution for those families who lost their homes, or jobs, or their retirement savings. In the political area it is always easy to criticize without offering a solution. # 3

The criticism from the Republican side of the isle came from Jenny Beth Martin, a co-founder of the Tea Party Patriots: "What we learned from TARP, the stimulus and the Detroit bailout is when big government, big business and big labor join forces at the taxpayers' expenses, it's the average citizen who is left out." # 4 What Martin did not consider was that TARP saved more than 900,000 jobs in the auto and related auto industries and over seven million homeowners received financial assistance and avoided foreclosure. The key questions, which none of the critics answered, is: (1) what is the function of government? and (2) what were their solutions for establishing economic recovery for the country?

Both Elizabeth Warren and Jenny Beth Martin have forgotten the answer to these questions. The answer to the first question came from a Democratic President: Franklin D. Roosevelt. In speaking about the Great Depression, he stated in 1938: "…if its business system does not provide employment and produce and distribute goods in such a way as to sustain an acceptable standard of living, democracy cannot survive." Roosevelt continued by saying, "Government has a final responsibility for the well-being of its citizenship. If private cooperative endeavor fails to provide work for willing hands and relief for the unfortunate, those suffering hardship from no fault of their own have a right to call upon the Government for aid; and a government worthy of its name must make a fitting response." # 5

George W Bush gave a similar explanation for his "all-in policy" that Roosevelt gave for his New Deal.

"I wished there were some way to hold individual firms to account while sparing the rest of the country. But every economist I trusted told me that was impossible." The well-being of Main Street was directly linked to the fate of Wall Street.

If credit markets remained frozen, the heaviest burdens would fall on American families with: steep drops in the value of retirement accounts, massive job losses, and further falling home values. On September 24, Bush gave a primetime address to the nation to explain the need for the rescue package. "I [understand]the frustration of responsible Americans who pay their mortgages on time, file their tax returns every April 15, and are reluctant to pay the cost of excesses on Wall Street," I said. "But given the situation we are facing, not passing a bill now would cost these Americans much more later." # 6

What George W. Bush and Barack Obama both demonstrated was great presidential leadership by having the vision to choose the correct path the country needed to take, even though it might have gone against some of their own political and personal values.

Theodore Roosevelt (TR) once defined his concept of the President as "steward of the people" and held that "it was not only his right but his duty to do anything that the needs of the nation demanded unless such action was forbidden by the Constitution or by laws." # 7

Theodore Roosevelt established the practice of a President interceding in a national economic crisis during the Anthracite Coal Strike of 1902. Roosevelt used the Presidency as an agent to guarantee a "just balance," or a Square Deal as he called it, between rival groups in society. Roosevelt became the first President in history to recognize the rights of labor in an industrial dispute.

The Anthracite Coal strike began when the United Mine Workers, under President John Mitchell, struck on May 12, 1902, for higher wages, union recognition, and an eight-hour day. Rather than follow the example of President Cleveland, who sent troops to break up the Pullman Strike of 1894, Roosevelt called representatives of the coal industry and the miners to the White House and asked both sides to agree to a new contract in the interest of the health and welfare of the nation.

When the coal industry balked at Roosevelt's proposal, he was prepared to take more drastic action. If Roosevelt could not persuade labor and management to accept arbitration voluntarily, he threatened to appoint a settlement board without their consent and arrange for the governor of Pennsylvania to request federal assistance to keep the peace. Roosevelt also intended to have federal troops "seize the mines and run them as a receiver for the government." Nowhere was the President's right to seize and operate private property in the Constitution. Without legal precedent or Congressional Legislation to justify his involvement Roosevelt moved forward and was successful in settling the strike. Roosevelt's actions mark the beginning of the modern Presidency. Before Roosevelt the idea of the federal government regulating any aspect of society (except for Andrew Jackson and his war on the Bank of the U.S.) was new and not fully accepted within society.

The Anthracite Coal Strike is only one example of Roosevelt's public policies which introduced the concept that the modern President and the national government are responsible to the people for the social and economic welfare of the nation. His actions during the strike expanded the role, power, and expectation of Presidential leadership in the minds of the public during the Progressive Movement. # 8

It is because of the actions and leadership demonstrated by both TR and FDR that the public now expects and demands that the federal government and the President take a leading role in solving any and all problems social or economic that face the nation and threatens the social and economic stability of the country.

An essential ingredient of public leadership is the ability to define the policy dilemmas facing the nation in terms of emerging historical situations. Only great leaders can see the emerging historical situations and have the **flexible vision** and **political courage** to exercise **good governance** by **adjusting** their personal and/or political values to what is in the best interest of the country. Even though this vision might lead in an unpopular direction with political consequences, it must be followed. What is important is not the success or failure of a President, but the future of this nation and the world economies. Our Founding Fathers felt that power was to be used by men of conscience, vision, and integrity for the common good. Therefore, power is a trust and public office an opportunity for public service. **Thus, from a point of view of public trust, leadership and from a political and historical standpoint, Bush and Obama had no choice---the U.S. government had to go all-in.**

Historically, the country has been fortunate in that the majority of men elected to the Presidency have been well supplied with political character. Successful Presidents at times have had to recognize that sometimes the restraints of party and ideology must be broken to achieve success for the nation. As President George H. W. Bush once said, "the most important thing about the office of the presidency is not the President , but upholding the dignity of the office of the presidency." In the years to come when the events of the 2007-2008 Financial Crisis are evaluated both Presidents George W. Bush and Barack Obama, will likely benefit from their leadership actions during this financial crisis.

As with the first financial crisis in 1792, the Financial Crisis in 2007-08 saw opposition developed against the government for bailing out the banks and being the lender-of-last-resort. In 1791-1792, Southerns Thomas Jefferson and James Madison opposed the creation of the Bank of the U.S. and Hamilton's efforts to use the Sinking Funds Committee to stabilize the economy (the Sinking Funds could be compared in some ways to the Federal Reserve Bank or a government savings account). It was a device to ensure creditors that the securities they purchased from the U.S. government would be redeemed. Jefferson and Madison felt the government's actions as well as Hamilton's were unconstitutional. Jefferson and Madison opposed all of Hamilton's financial programs because they felt Hamilton programs would perpetuate the interest of the wealthy and would provide little benefit to the common man and farming interests. These hostilities over Hamilton's programs in Congress later led to the development of our two-party system. The hostility against TARP produced the same social and economic arguments that Hamilton's programs produced. As mentioned, Elizabeth Warren's statement, like that of Jefferson and Madison's, argued that bank and debt relief programs only bailed out Wall Street and the wealthy and did little for the common man.

For some of Bush's critics, the cause of the financial panic and meltdown was his Administration's desire to increase home ownership for low-income and first-time buyers. The term "ownership society" is a slogan for a model of society promoted by President George W. Bush. The concept of an ownership society is based on the values of personal responsibility, economic liberty, and the owning of property---particularly your own home. The ownership society as proposed by Bush also included specific models of health care and social security.

Bush's home ownership policy is the story of a well-intended policy gone awry. Although homeownership was an important issue in the early development of our country, Bush's homeownership society is founded on different principles than the original "stake in society theory" that developed in our early history. Homeownership is not only historically a part of the American Dream, but the idea has played a major role in the historical development of our society. In order to vote in the early 1600's and 1700's a person had to have a certain amount of personal wealth which later included land ownership. As people moved west to the frontier region, there was plenty of land thus universal male suffrage soon became the political standard in the West. Between 1812 -1821, six western states entered the Union with constitutions providing for universal white male suffrage or a close approximation. The development in the western states put pressure on eastern states to follow suit by dropping property requirements for voting and holding office. Thus, "the stake in society theory" or homeownership was part of a steppingstone process in developing democracy in our society.

Bush's home ownership society is more a reflection of his personal beliefs, values, and moral code rather than ideology or politics. Bush's beliefs are centered around what he describes as compassionate conservatism. "Compassionate conservatism offers a new paradigm for how the government can and should intervene in the economy. It begins with a long-lost premise about human behavior: economics, by itself, is not what changes lives. For decades the government has focused only on material well-being, ignoring the passions and convictions that make life worth living." # 9 Bush's compassionate conservatism is based on:

"The creed that promotes social progress through individual change". Bush believed the United States had too many needy citizens for whom the American dream was out of reach. "Compassionate Conservatism" is a conservatism that cares about them and makes a concerted effort to help them bring lasting change into their lives. # 10 (Ibid page xi-xii) In justifying his home ownership policy Bush stated in June of 2002: "My approach to broadening homeownership focuses on empowering people to help themselves, and to help one another. These important initiatives will accomplish their purpose because Americans, working together and taking responsibility for one another, will make this great country even greater." # 11 The idea that the well-being of individuals is directly related to their ability to control their own lives and wealth, rather than relying on government transfer payments is the foundation of "compassionate conservatism" and Bush's personal values and moral code.

During the colonial period and during the formative years of the United States the stake in society theory was quite common. The theory was that those who owned land would have a stake in society and would value social order and stability and therefore should have the right to vote. Bush felt by owning their home people would have a stake in society.

In his book Decision Points Bush expresses his thoughts on the housing boom.

"At the height of the housing boom, homeownership hit an all-time high of almost 70 percent. I had supported policies to expand homeownership, including down-payment assistance for low-income and first-time buyers. I was pleased to see the ownership society grow. But the exuberance of the moment masked the underlying risk. Together, the global pool of cash, easy monetary policy, a booming housing market, insatiable appetite for mortgage-backed assets, complexity of Wall Street financial engineering, and leveraging of financial institutions created a house of cards. This precarious structure was fated to collapse as soon as the underlying card—the nonstop growth of housing prices—was pulled out. **That was clear in retrospect. But very few saw it at the time, including me."** * # 12

It is clear from the above quote that President Bush understands the exact cause of the Financial Crisis and that his quote could be used as an outline for this book.

Bush admits that his personal philosophy or beliefs played a role in creating the housing boom. Did he or members of his administration create the financial panic and meltdown---the answer is NO. Although some would like to label them as being responsible for the crisis. But Bush and members of his administration should have seen that allowing first-time buyers to purchase a home without paying a down payment and closing costs created a situation where they had no stake in the home and thus would be more prone to walk away if and when times get tough.

Was the Bush ownership policy a bad policy? Keith Hennessey, Bush's chief economic adviser answered the question in an article in the "The New York Times on 12/21/2008", "I would not say too much emphasis on expanding home ownership, I would say not enough early focus on easy lending practices." # 13

What can also be said about President Bush and his administration's handling of the Financial Crisis is that they created the tools and laid the foundation for the economic recovery that occurred during the Obama administration. To Obama's credit he followed through on Bush's "all-in policy" and continued to build on the foundation Bush created.

In December of 2008, Fox News asked Bush if he was worried about being the Herbert Hoover of the 21st century. "No," Bush replied. "I will be known as somebody who saw a problem and put the chips on the table to prevent the economy from collapsing;" A president must do whatever it takes--within the law--to protect the American people. I remain at peace with the decision I made as president." # 14 This quote explains the significance of Bush's "all-in policy."

As with the 1990 congressional budget crises and the Financial Crisis of 2007-2008, historical events have created circumstances or opportunities for Presidents to expand their influence. The Civil War, the Progressive Movement, and the Great Depression are just a few classic examples that allowed Presidents Abraham Lincoln, Theodore Roosevelt, and Franklin D. Roosevelt the opportunity to accomplish great deeds and demonstrate strong leadership. Each period of Presidential dominance in American history has been marked by a special set of circumstances such as a war or a compelling national problem that convinced Congress and the public that bold Presidential actions were needed. Thus, great Presidential leadership has come about not as a result of Presidents creating the historical events, but as a result of their actions during times of crisis.

President George H. W. Bush made this point clear in a 1988 discussion with Doug Wead (a campaign staffer for President Bush) "…the Presidency provides an incomparable opportunity for moral leadership…" and that "public service has been hurt by individuals who lack the judgment or character to put the public's business above their own self-interest." President John F. Kennedy might have referred to the actions of both Bush 41 and 43 during their respective crises as a "profile in courage." But both father and son would probably have said with characteristic humility, that they were just doing what they were elected to do.

The question is, did Presidents Bush and Obama demonstrate that kind of leadership? The answer to that question will differ for each reader and only the reader can decide. It is hoped this book has provided an objective perspective and given additional background information and insight into the complexities of the economic and financial problems facing the country, as well as the problems and decisions a leader must face in times of crises.

The key question the reader needs to consider is: what should a responsible government do in an asset bubble? There appear to be three choices: (1) The government should attempt to prick and slowly deflate the asset bubble before it becomes too large and bursts. (2) The government should recognize the peak of an asset bubble is difficult to determine until it bursts; thus, the government should wait watchfully and then move quickly when the bubble bursts to contain and minimize the bad economic effects that might ensue. Or (3) should the government do nothing and just let the free market play out?

History seems to indicate that when financial systems are on the brink of collapse, bailouts were deemed to be the lesser of two evils.

Historical hindsight always makes the correct decisions look easy, but during a crisis or the heat of battle the path to victory is not always so clear, because in most cases there is limited time and incomplete information to make the correct decision. This is particularly true when the cause of the crisis has developed over a long period of time. What has to be relied upon are the intelligence, character, and leadership abilities of those in charge of finding the correct path to victory.

The purpose of this book is to demonstrate how the Financial Crisis developed over a prolonged period of time, and how President George W. Bush's pragmatic vision, leadership and political will laid the foundation for economic recovery. Just as important as President Bush's vision and leadership skills was the ability of President Obama and his administration to build upon the financial foundation and reforms established under the Bush administration.

References by Chapters for the 2007-2008 Financial Crisis

Introduction

1. Ostrander/Bush George W. "Read My Lips: No New Taxes" Butte College Press , 1999, p 50
2. Geithner Timothy, Stress Test (Crown Publishers New York 2010) p 138
3. Bush, George W. Decision Points. (Crown Publishers NeYork2010) p 458
4. Ibid p.459
5. Keith Hennessey, Deputy Assistant to President Bush for Economic Policy and Deputy Director, National Economic Council, Interview, August 25, 2023.
6. Ibid p.458-459
7. Keith Hennessey, Deputy Assistant to President Bush for Economic Policy and Deputy Director, National Economic Council, Interview, August 25, 2023
8. New York Times, "Pretty Good for Government Work" 11/17/2010
9. Geithner Timothy, Stress Test (Crown Publishers New York 2010) p 144
10. Ibid.
11. Wessel, David In Fed We Trust (Crown Publishers New York 2009) p 256
12. Geithner Timothy, Stress Test (Crown Publishers New York 2010) p 220

13. Americas (Topic/Americas), "The Financial Crisis, but Nobody's Going to Jail", by Avi Asher-Schapiro, April 11,2016.

14. Reuters U.S. Legal News March 4, 2020 (http://www.npr.org/sectopms/tje two-way/2016/04/00 by Jim Zarroli

15. Reuters, "Banks have paid $321 billion in fines since the financial crisis:" BCG, by Kevin Coombs, January 19,2017

16. Violation Tracker (https://www.goodjobsfist.org/violation-tracker) Philip Mattera is the Research Director at Good Jobs First and was director of Corporate Research for this project. Published July 21,2022

Section: 1 Legislative Impact

1. The New York Times, "Affordable Housing, Racial Isolation By the Editorial Board, June 29,2015.
2. New York Post, "The Real Scandal" Stan Liebowitz.
3. 12 U.S. Code & 4501 congressional findings I LII/ Legal Information Institute.
4. New York Post, "The Real Scandal" by Stan Liebowitz.
5. New York Times, "A Deregulator Looks Back, Unsawed", 11/17/08.
6. Ibid.
7. Money Wise, July 30, 2024, by Vishesh Raisinghanl
8. The Financial Crisis Inquiry Report National Commission on the Causes of the Financial and Economic Crisis in the United States, GPO. February 25, 2011.
9. Bernanke, Ben S. "Fed Chairman Bernanke Confirms to Menendez That Community Reinvestment Act is not to Blame for Foreclosure Crisis" (http://www.menendez.senate.gov/newsroom/press/fed-chairman. December 2, 2008.

10. Yellen, Janet L. "Opening Remarks, 2008 National Interagency Community Reinvestment Conference", March 31,2008.

11. CNN, "Countrywide defrauded Fannie and Freddie, jury rules." By James O'Toole, October 23,2013.

12. Business Insider by John Carney June 27, 2009

13. Bernanke, Ben S., *Fed Chairman Ben Bernanke gave a speech entitled: The Crisis and the Policy Response* Wall Street Journal, *January 2009*

14. Wall Street Journal, "Rethinking Capitalism's Contours", October 20, 2008

15. Wall Street Journal, "Central-Bank Digital Currencies are Coming—Whether Countries are Ready or Not," by Christopher Mims, January 16, 2023.

16. The Palm Beach Research Group, "The Biden Shock of 2023", September 18, 2023.

Section: 2 The Creation of New Economic Tools

1. John Kenneth Galbraith, Money: Whence it came, Where It Went, (Houghton Mifflin2001) p 305.
2. Ibid, p 3.
3. Ibid, John K. Galbraith, Interview with Brian Lamb, November 13, 1994.
4. John Kenneth Galbraith, Money: Whence it came, Where It Went, (Houghton Mifflin Harcourt 2001) p 21.
5. Time Magazine, "One Bad Bond March 2009, pp. 30-31

Section: 3 Globalization its Impact on Global and Domestic Economies

1. "Joint Statement by the government of the Russian Federation and the Central Bank of the Russian Federation on the

Exchange Rate Policy", August 17,1998. http://www.cbr.reu/eng/press/JPOMT.htm,

2. The Economist, "The monetary-policy maze" April 25, 2009, p 74.
3. Washington Post, "Greenspan's Age of Tranquility," September 24, 2007, p 31.
4. Washington Post, February 5, 2006, p 7

Section: 4 Alan Greenspan and the Federal Reserve Policies

1. John Kenneth Galbraith, Money: Whence it came, Where It Went, (Houghton Mifflin Harcourt 2001) p 26.
2. Alan Greenspan, The Age OF Turbulence, Penguin Books, pp 256-257, 2007
3. Yahoo Finance, Greenspan denies blame for crisis, amidst "flaw". October 23, 2008.
4. Alan Greenspan, The Age OF Turbulence, Penguin Books, pp 256-257, 2007
5. Ibid.
6. Businessweek magazine, "Is the Housing Bubble about to Burst?" Coy, Peter: et al., July 19, 2004.
7. Washington Post, Nell Henderson, February 5, 2006, page 7
8. Geithner Timothy, Stress Test (Crown Publishers New York 2010) p 138
9. Ostrander, Dan, American History—The Relevant Issues, A History of the United States from 1877 to the Present Vol. II, Butte College Press, 2004, p 125.

Section: 5 The Rating Agencies

1. Cantor, Richard; Packer, Frank [Summer-fall 1994] "The

credits rating industry"' Federal Reserve Bank of New York Quarterly Review. Federal Reserve Bank of New York pp.1-26. ISSN 0147-6580.

2. Ibid.
3. Mclean Bethany and Joe Nocera, All The Devils Are Here, The Hidden History of the Financial Crisis, *(Penguin Books pp 117-118, 2010)*
4. Yahoo Finance—business Insider, 2011
5. Associated Press, New York Yahoo finances, 6/3/2010.
6. New York Times, Whitefish Bay School Board, 11/3/2008.
7. Ibid.
8. Senator Carl Levin, Market Watch, April 23,2010.
9. The New York Times, "Hey, S.E.C. That Escape Hatch Is Still Open" by Gretchen Mortenson, March 5, 2011.
10. Alan Greenspan, The Age OF Turbulence, Penguin Books, pp 256- 257, 2007

Section: 6 The Greed of Main Street and Wall Street

1. Ostrander, Dan, American History—The Relevant Issues, A History of the United States from 1877 to the Present Vol. II, Butte College Press, 2004, p 132.

Section: 7 The Role of Fannie Mae

1. "Assessing the Public Costs and Benefits of Fannie Mae and Freddie Mac/ congressional Budget Office" www.cbo.gov/doc.cfm? Index=13&type=0) Cbo.gov. 1996-05-01.
2. Washington Post, June 10,2008, "How HUD Mortgage Policy Fed the Crisis" by Carol D. Leonning, June 10,2008.
3. Mclean Bethany and Joe Nocera, All The Devils Are Here, The

Hidden History of the Financial Crisis, *(Penguin Books p181, 2010)*

4. New York Times, September 30, 1999, "Fannie Mae Eases Credit to Aid Mortgage Lending" by Steven Holmes.
5. "Fed Chief Warns of a Risk to Taxpayers", (http://query.nytimes.com/gst/fullgage.html), New York Times, 2004.

Chapter: 2 The Solution

1. Richard Nixon, No More Vietnams, (Arbor House New York 1985) p 224
2. Bush, George W. Decision Points. (Crown Publishers NeYork2010) p 459
3. Geithner Timothy, Stress Test (Crown Publishers New York 2010) p 67
4. President George W. Bush, Conference in South Carolina in October 2018 attended by my wife Dawn and myself.

Section 1: The Banking and Investment Programs (BIP)

1. ProPublica, Bailout Tracker, Emergency Economic Stabilization Act-Capital Purchase Program, 2019.
2. *ProPublica, Bailout Tracker, Emergency Economic Stabilization Act-Asset Guarantee Program, 2019.*
3. *ProPublica, Bailout Tracker, Emergency Economic Stabilization Act-Targeted Investment Program, 2019.*
4. *ProPublica, Bailout Tracker, Emergency Economic Stabilization Act, Community Development Capital Initiative (CDCI), 2019.*

Section 2: Credit Markets

1. ProPublica, Bailout Tracker, Emergency Economic Stabilization Public-Private Investment Program, 2019.

2. Press Release, Federal Reserve Board, December 19, 2008.

3. ProPublica, Bailout Tracker, Emergency Economic Stabilization Public-Private Investment Program, 2019.

Section 3: American International Group (AIG)

1. Federal Reserve Bank of New York, Report--Actions related to AIG,

2. The U.S. Department of the Treasury, The Official Web Site of the U.S. Government---Report on: Investment in American International Group (AIG), March 2013.

Section 4: Automotive Industry Financing Program (AIFP)

1. ProPublica, Bailout Tracker, Automotive Industry Financing Program, 2019.

2. congressional Research Service, The Role of TARP Assistance in the Restructuring of General Motors pp 5-13.

3. ProPublica, Bailout Tracker, Automotive Industry Financing Program, 2019.

4. Ibid.

5. ProPublica, Bailout Tracker, Automotive Supply Support Program, 2019.

6. Ibid.

Section: 5 The Affordable Housing Programs

1. An official website of the United States Government, U.S. Department of the Treasury, Hardest Hit Fund (HHF), 2024.

2. *"The "End of the Affair"* ***https://www.econmist.com/world/unitedstates/displaystory.cfm*** */story id=12637090. The Economist 2008-10-30. Retrieved 2009-02-27.*

3. *Ibid.*
4. Wikipedia (the Free Encyclopedia) Home Affordable Refinance Program, p 1.
5. ProPublica, Bailout Tracker, Housing and Economic Recovery Act of 2008, Bailout Recipients, August 18, 2022.

Section: 6 The Federal Reserve and the Liquidity Crisis

1. The Journal of Financial Crises, volume 2, Issue 2: The Federal Reserve's Financial Crisis Response D: Commercial Paper Market Facilities by Andrew Metrick Yale University Pages 118-121.
2. *"Treasury Announces Expiration of Guarantee Program for Money Market Fhttp://www.treasury.gov/press-center/press-releases/Pages/tg293.aspx.*

Chapter 3: The Profit/Loss and Final TARP Balance Sheet

the congressional Budget Office in their Troubled Asset Relief Program-September 2023; *Lombard Street A Description of the Money Market by Walter Bagehot 1962 Richard E. Irwin, Inc. Homewood, Illinois, pp. 22-23.*

1. The Atlantic, The Villain by Roger Lowenstein, April 2012 p.53.
2. Associated Press, April 1. 2010, "Geithner: Disparity in recovery 'deeply unfair'."

Chapter: 4 Conclusion

1. Associated Press, April 1. 2010, "Geithner: Disparity in recovery 'deeply unfair'." (Budgetary Effects of The Troubled Asset Relief Program page # 23 page 301)
2. *Pimco Managing Director Neel Kaskari told Squawk Box "I think*

unemployment would have been 25 percent or higher without TARP. We're talking Great Depression levels". (Jobless Rate would be 25% Without TARP: Kashkari by Barbara Stcherbatcheff CNBC April 26, 210)

3. *The New York Times, U.S. Declares Bank and Auto Bailouts Over, and Profitable by Jonathan Weisman Dec.19 2014.*
4. *Ibid.*
5. *Ostrander, American History—The Relevant Issues: A History of the United States from 1877 to the Present P 125)*
6. Bush, George W. Decision Points. (Crown Publishers NeYork2010) p *460.*
7. *Ostrander/Bush "Read My Lips: No New Taxes" Butte College Press, 1999, p 2.*
8. *Ostrander, American History—The Relevant Issues: A History of the United States from 1877 to the Present P 125)*
9. *Compassionate Conservatism by Marvin Olasky with a foreword by George W. Bush, The Free Press, New York, 2000, Dust Jacket.*
10. *Ibid. pp. xi-xii.*
11. *National-Laredo Morning Times—Sunday June 16,2002 page 13A)*
12. Bush, George W. Decision Points. (Crown Publishers NeYork2010) p 459.
13. *"The New York Times," Bush drive for home ownership fueled housing bubble, by Lo Becker, Sherry Gay, and Stephen Labaton. 12/21/2008.*
14. *Ibid.*

www.ingramcontent.com/pod-product-compliance
Lightning Source LLC
LaVergne TN
LVHW022054200926
848481LV00003B/901